Of

YOUR

OWN

WAY

Lifting Yourself to Higher Ground

LYNN ALLEN-JOHNSON

Foreword by Best-Selling Author Denis Waitley

Praise for
Getting Out of
Your Own Way

"An important book for anyone who wants to succeed in their home-based business! It outlines powerful strategies that will help you and your team to succeed bringing with it the opportunity to finally enjoy an exciting balanced life."

> — Steve Swartz & Pat Berry
> Authors of *"The Invisible Millionaire"*

"Brilliant! A life changing piece of writing! In *Getting Out Of Your Own Way* Lynn Allen-Johnson walks you through a journey of self-discovery and personal fulfillment. I believe that this book may be one of the most significant step by step manuals to reaching your full potential in the home-based business industry, and that is no small statement."

> — Dave Ogunnaike
> Author of *"Millionaire Genius"*

"Those of us who've had the privilege to hear Lynn speak about leadership, perseverance and the steps needed to *Raise Yourself to Higher Ground* intimately realize her many magnificent gifts and commitment to inspire and add value to the lives of others. *Getting Out Of Your Own Way* is filled with compelling insight, real-life illustrations, and practical to do's. This book is for anyone who aspires to build a dynamic, productive and a financially rewarding home-based business."

— Dr. Cynthia Barnett
Author of *"Stop Singing the Blues"*

"A winner. It's the best, a perfect guide to turn you and your team into record setting All-Stars."

— Dr. Tony Smithlin
Founder - *Smithlin Chiropractic*

"If you're serious about changing your life, the concepts and ideas in this book will blow you away."

— Steve Colwell
President and Founder *Colwell Enterprise*

"If you're looking for plain theoretical concepts and philosophical antidotes, you will not find them here. All you'll find in *Getting Out Of Your Own Way* are practical examples of how to develop a roadmap that can actually take you to your desired destination. This is a highly readable, content-pact book that clearly comes from Lynn's heart with sincerity and enthusiasm."

> — Mike Delevante
> President—*Granite and Tile Source*

"As a lifelong friend of Lynn's for over 20 years, I've witnessed her journey and observed as her dreams came true to fruition. A must read for you to discover that "all you need lies within you."

> — Ginny Sorenson

"At a time where individuals, families and organizations are struggling to produce measurable results in their lives, Lynn Allen-Johnson provides an empowering philosophy for life that is also the best opportunity of achieving success in business. This book combines a perfect blend of wisdom, compassion, and practical experience."

> — Mike Ray
> President—*Intertel Communications*
> click2wealth.com

"My dear friend, Lynn Allen-Johnson has proven her ability as a leader through inspiration, motivation and a genuine heart for others. She has lifted herself to higher ground and will guide you on your journey to achieve your dreams..."

— Deborah Phillips

"One of the greatest attributes of Lynn Allen-Johnson is that she challenges you to grow as a person and to reach your true potential. *Getting Out Of Your Own Way* offers practical steps to help you become the high achiever you were meant to be. This book will inspire you to overcome whatever obstacles you are facing on a personal and professional level. After reading this book you'll be highly motivated to encourage others and add value to their lives. I highly endorse Lynn's principles for success and believe this is a "must read" book.

— Brian Klemmer
Best selling author of *"If How-To's were enough We would all be SKINNY, RICH & HAPPY"*

"Lynn Allen-Johnson's *Getting Out Of Your Own Way* provides platinum quality business advise for working on your personal development or growth while simultaneously building a successful business."

> — Kimberly A. Wilson
> President Kimberly's Jewelry

"At a time where individuals, families and organizations are struggling to produce measurable results in their lives, Lynn Allen-Johnson provides an empowering philosophy for life that is also the best opportunity for achieving success in business. This book combines a perfect blend of wisdom, compassion and practical experience and I believe that everyone should read it, as it has the power to change lives."

> — Dr. Ladd McNamara, Author of
> *"The Cholesterol Conspiracy"*

Getting Out Of

YOUR
OWN
WAY

For information, write to:
e2iBooks
1800 Pembrooke Drive 3rd Floor
Orlando, FL 32810

The **e2iBooks** name and logo are registered trademarks of **e2iBooks**

Ever thought about writing a book, visit our website at:
www.e2ibooks.com
or email us at: publishing@e2ibooks.com

Printed in the United States of America

First edition **e2iBooks** printing: September 2005

Library of Congress Cataloging-in-Publication Data

Allen-Johnson, Lynn, 1947-
Getting out of your own way : lifting yourself to higher ground / by
Lynn Allen-Johnson.-- 1st ed.p. cm.
ISBN 0-9763177-1-0 (pbk. : alk. paper)
1. Self-actualization (Psychology) I. Title.
BF637.S4A5735 2005
158.1--dc22
2005022282

ISBN # 0-9763177-1-0

Getting Out Of

YOUR OWN WAY

Lifting Yourself to Higher Ground

LYNN ALLEN-JOHNSON

Foreword by Best-Selling Author Denis Waitley

Dedication

I dedicate this book to my Father who died when I was 16. And although for way to short a time, I was so blessed to have him in my life. Thank you for coloring with me when I was spotted with German measles. Thank you for the courage you showed even in the end and thank you for your unselfish love for us all. You are with me always.

I dedicate this book to my loving family. They teach me every day that I am wealthy beyond measure because I have them in my life. And to my husband I want to say thank you for believing in me as I've traveled this road of self discovery. Thank you for the sacrifices that I know you've made in order to allow me spread my wings and soar with the eagles. I love you.

I also want to make a special dedication to Dr. Myron Wentz whose vision has allowed me to unlock the sleeping giant within me. I have discovered and am living my true purpose...What a gift...

To My Readers

We've all been born with the potential for living a fulfilled, happy, and enjoyable life. Some of us have achieved extraordinary success in business and in life, some of us have watched others achieve it, and still others have wondered *will it ever happen for me...*

If you're one of those asking "Where is the success for me?" or "When is it my turn?" read on and allow me to help you awaken the sleeping giant inside of you that feels stuck, dissatisfied, frustrated, and afraid. My hope for each of you is that my words will awaken you to the fulfillment, happiness, and joy you've been yearning for and that you once again will dare to dream and begin exploring life's possibilities...

Don't just read the words but digest their meaning over and over as you apply them to your life. Please know that the "yes" deep inside of you is your God given power to have a fulfilled satisfying and abundant life. You deserve it!

Enjoy...

Acknowledgements

I would like to thank my daughter, Jami, for caring enough to send me these amazing products, for without her none of this would be possible. Little did I know when I opened that box that the entire direction of my life would change.

I would like to say a special thank you to my amazing team as I wouldn't be living this dream if not for them. They have enriched my life and inspire me to achieve. They have shown courage and commitment while fighting for their dreams, and every day I am thankful for my success which comes from making a difference in their lives. Happiness is watching them grow…

I would also like to thank Christian Warren and his phenomenal team at e2ibooks for the incredible work they did in assisting me to put my voice to print…I could never have done it without them…

Table of Contents

Foreword

Every once in a while someone comes along who renews your faith in the human spirit and gives you courage to believe you can face your fears and rise above your environmental circumstances to realize your highest aspirations.

Lynn Allen-Johnson is one of those rare individuals who lights up every room she enters, and enters every heart she touches. I have watched her incredible journey toward self-fulfillment these past few years with awe and respect. At first, I viewed her as a caring friend and associate. Before long I could sense that there was something different and special about this remarkable woman that would impact thousands of people all striving for better health and personal freedom.

Every time I hear her speak to an audience about her life adventure, I am confronted with a torrent of emotions. On one hand, I am laughing with joy responding to her unassuming directness and humor as she describes her often arduous climb to the top of her profession. On the other hand, I am quickly wiping the tears welling up in my eyes caused by the sheer intensity and spirit-lifting account of her struggles with her own insecurities and doubts. What makes watching her and listening to her so real, is that her own tears and joys overflow before our eyes, and no one is left immune and uninvolved in what she is describing. That's the one word I want to convey to you as you scan these pages: The word **REAL**. Not as in reality TV, but real as in real life.

Now we have the pleasure of reading her innermost thoughts and feelings up front, close and personal. Platform presentations are stimulating. But too soon the words are forgotten and we are left with simply a warm feeling about the speaker and what he or she said. That's why books are so important as stepping stones to the stars in our lives. We can read and re-read the paragraphs. We can underline our favorite passages. We can keep the book on our desk or bedside table and re-visit it as often as we like to gain new insights or positive reinforcement in trying times.

Lynn-Allen Johnson's book can give you the change you want, if you will give it the chance. Dare to dream with her as she declares her vision and mission in life. Join her in defining you own leadership role in your family and on your team. Travel with her as she helps you confirm that you are driving the right vehicle up the mountain and let her discover with you, what matters most along the way.

Lynn's amazing saga reflects the progress she has made in just a few years, from a woman who started her own home-based business just to use the products and who prayed that no one would ask her about the business opportunity because she didn't want anything to do with it; to one of top leaders and income earners representing the company as an independent associate. She is truly a walking, breathing example of the "Acres of Diamonds" principle, that happiness lies right under your eyes, in your own mind, with your own family and friends, right in your own backyard.

This book will also assist you in doing the right things consistently to further your business and personal goals, and perhaps, most importantly, the critical steps you need to take in developing your own leadership team. If there's one underlying theme throughout her life and throughout the pages that follow, it is that it is impossible to succeed in isolation in today's world. You may think "success is a do-it-yourself project," and certainly being self-determined and proactive are keys to achievement. However, Lynn will ensure that you always remember that "success is a do-it-for-and-with others project."

As my personal tribute to Lynn's first published work, I've dedicated a little verse that sums up how I feel about her and the contents of this book:

Living is giving your best self away
Living is serving with grace every day
You'll know that you've won, when your friends say,
"It's true!"
"I like who I am, when I'm around you."
"You look for the best in the me that you see"
"And you help me become all I can be"
Some people think that success is in "getting"
But there's one of God's laws they keep on forgetting
And this is the one you can live and believe
The more that you give, the more you'll receive

— Dr. Denis Waitley, author
"The Seeds of Greatness"

Introduction

Have you ever wondered why some people are successful in life and others are not? Or, more importantly, have you ever wondered if you have what it takes to be one of the people who are successful?

My belief is that you have within you the seeds to success and the ability to make your every dream come true. We all have it within us. The reason people aren't as successful as they want to be is not because they lack ability, it's because they lack the ability to unleash their ability. Let me be loud and clear – the biggest stumbling block that holds people back from success is themselves. But, that's all going to change with this book, because by the time you're finished, you will have learned how to "Get Out Of Your Own Way." I did it, and so can you.

I've had many experiences in my life and have created many successes for myself. Through hard work and dedication, I've brought myself to a place where I'm truly living my dream. But it wasn't always like this. In fact, a few short years ago I was just another average person standing on the outside of the banquet of success, pressing my nose to the glass, and wondering what the difference was between all of those people living fulfilling, successful lives and me.

Thanks to a few miracles and a lot of hard work I found a powerful secret to success – and in this book I'm going to share it with you. And while this book will certainly help you "Get Out Of Your Own Way," it also offers so much more. You'll get a step-by-step roadmap to building a successful business. The focus is on building a Network Marketing business, but the core principles apply equally to any successful business or venture.

This hopefully won't be the only book you read on your road to success, but it could possibly be the most powerful. It's designed to help you at every stage of your journey... from getting in touch with your dream to developing your leadership skills, from building and managing a team to executing a business model that works. And, of course, how to reap the rewards of all your efforts.

If you're just beginning on your journey, this book is a solid roadmap that will take you from your very first step to the pinnacle of your success. If you're already on your journey, this book can act as a guidepost to refocus your direction and an opportunity to rekindle the spark that drives your vision. If you've already achieved great success, this book can help you map out your next adventure in life.

The philosophies, principles, and steps you'll find in the coming pages are based on my personal experiences, along with the experiences of the countless people I've been fortunate enough to meet along the way. The path I've mapped out is proven to work. The steps are simple yet powerful. Over and over again, people have used the wisdom and principles in this book to realize their dreams. You can too.

"Getting Out Of Your Own Way" holds within it the keys you need to make your dreams come true. It has the potential to change your life, but only if you're ready. So, if you are, buckle your seat belts and hold on for the ride of your life. You're about to learn what it takes to survive and thrive in this business...on your own terms. You're about to experience the priceless joy and fulfillment that comes from following the most important path of all in life...your own.

"There is no duty so much underrated as the duty of being happy."

— Robert Louis Stevenson

Chapter One
Daring To Dream

The first spark of this book came as I was sitting on the deck of my beach home, drinking a glass of cabernet, and watching a bird glide inches above a wave gently rolling onto the bleached white sand of the summer shore. Soaking up the late afternoon sun while marveling at the aquamarine water of the Florida coast, I began to wonder about that bird. Why, with all of its freedom, would that beautiful bird choose to be at this beach at this very moment? I quickly realized I was asking the wrong question. The real question was "Why weren't there more birds here?" Why wasn't the beach filled with birds? More importantly, why were some birds willing to settle for living in dirty city alleys or on non-descript rooftops, when they could soar in the gentle breeze of a tropical beach? What made some birds choose squalor and other birds choose paradise?

Instinctively, I realized I already knew the answer. Only a few short years before that day on the beach, I was living an ordinary, plain wrap life. I was living paycheck to paycheck, just getting by. My job was okay. I wasn't miserable. But I wasn't happy either. I was just passing time—and without much to show for it. I was 51-years-old and living in a small, two bedroom apartment. Truth was, I wasn't looking for anything more than what I already had. I suppose I had unconsciously made the choice to live on the "non-descript rooftop," never dreaming of reaching for the "paradise" of a brighter world or a grander life. I can hardly call it a choice. To me it just was—and I accepted it. Like those birds scratching out a meager existence from dumpster scraps, I didn't know any other way of life existed. And even if I had an inclination that there was more to life, I didn't for one second believe I could ever find it. I didn't believe I could change my destiny. But guess what? I did change my destiny. I switched gears and gave my life a total overhaul. And it wasn't hard to do.

As I breathed in the crisp sea air on that perfect afternoon at the beach I had to smile at my life. I had my dream home. I traveled often. I was making more money than I ever thought possible. Best of all, I had control of my schedule and my life, and I used that control to spend my days doing what I loved most—enjoying time with my children and grandchildren. I was living a life I loved, and I'm still living it today. In just a few short years I had completely turned my life around. I literally changed my destiny. And I did it by making a simple choice.

I woke up one day and decided to break the chains of mediocrity, the business as usual cycle of living paycheck to paycheck, renting an apartment and scheduling my life at the mercy of a job I couldn't afford to give up. I made the conscious choice to not just change my destiny…but to create a new destiny. And today, I'm a living example of what we can all do when we learn the power of choice, followed by the simple decision to take action. I'm a living example of what we can do when we Dare To Dream.

I made another choice on the balcony that day. I vowed to spend the rest of my life teaching others how to change their destinies as well. I wanted to help others feel as good about their lives as I did about mine. And the truth is, you don't really get something until you give it away and share it with others.

I should also mention here that while I said I changed my destiny, in truth, I don't think destinies even exist— certainly not in the way we think, not as something thrust upon us unwillingly. Rather, our only destinies are the lives we imagine, then willingly create for ourselves. I created my destiny, the life of my dreams…and now I can help you create your own destiny—the life of your dreams. I assure you, if I can do it, you can too.

The Joy Of Despair

> *"Discontent is the first step in the progress of a man or a nation."*
> — Oscar Wilde

My journey began years ago. I woke up one day as I usually did—lacking energy, motivation, and a sense of purpose. I was caught in that seemingly endless struggle to figure out how my life had turned out so mundane and boring. Again, I don't mean to say I was miserable…I wasn't. I just wasn't happy. But finally, after many years of being "not happy," I was beginning to wonder if there was more to life than what I grudgingly woke up to every day. I couldn't help but feel that something was missing from my life. Like so many other seekers, I had plodded along for years, not even realizing that I didn't like my life. It never occurred to me that there was any other way of living.

I still don't know why, but on that day my thoughts and emotions began to bubble to the surface. Maybe they had been working their way up for years. Maybe they had always been there and I had ignored them. In any case, the discontent rose to the surface, and for the first time I really felt it. It was painful and a blessing at the same time. I imagine it was a gift from God, but it wasn't anything spectacular—no near-death experience or sudden epiphany—just a simple question. "Is there more to life?"

At first, I didn't know what to do with the question. I didn't have an answer to the discontent. Still just feeling anything at all was a breath of fresh air. I felt alive. Oh sure, I was scared. I wanted desperately to gravitate back towards the status quo. I did everything I could to recapture the safety of my everyday routine. But it was too late. The seed had been planted. A tiny window of light opened up in my life and the question jumped through the window and straight into my consciousness—"Is there more to life?"

One thing I've learned for certain is that God doesn't give us a question without also giving us the answer. This time the answer came quickly. I didn't realize at the time what a great miracle it would be. Like so many deserving individuals before me, I was about to be given a life changing gift. Of course, like most gifts, I would have to open it myself.

Life Is Difficult

> *"One day, in retrospect, the years of struggle will strike you as the most beautiful."*
> — Sigmund Freud

It was during that same fateful week that I happened to pick up a copy of M. Scott Peck's famous book, *The Road*

Less Traveled. In his very first sentence, Peck said it all, "Life is difficult."

While certainly not the most uplifting and motivational words ever written, it was in that one moment, reading that one small sentence when I began to feel an enormous sense of calm begin to surround me. It was as if a huge weight had been lifted off my shoulders. Suddenly my personal, financial, and relationship challenges didn't seem so huge.

For so long I thought that to reach for the stars and pursue a path of success meant enormous amounts of hard work along with insurmountable challenges and obstacles. In fact, I think part of the reason I never tried to achieve great success was because I didn't want to face that difficulty. It just seemed too hard, too overwhelming. But guess what? My life was hard anyway. Yes, success is difficult, but so is mediocrity and failure. Let's face it—life *is* difficult. And once we can all agree on that, it's time to deal with the fact and do something about it. In other words, if life is going to be difficult no matter what we choose, why not choose success? Why not choose to be happy? Why not choose to live the life of our dreams? It seems so simple. But why doesn't everyone do it? The answer is just as simple. It's because they don't know they can.

As a human race, as a culture, as a society, as individuals… we've lost touch with our power, our abilities, our willingness to take risks and dream big. Truth is, many of us have forgotten or, worse, never knew we could Dare To Dream. Most of us have let outside events and influences shape our lives. We've listened to and believed the roadblocks that society puts in front of us. There's a recession. There's inflation. We need a Master's Degree to get ahead. We can't have a family *and* a career. It's tough to be a woman, a minority, young, old.

We've been sold a bill of goods when all along we knew that success has nothing to do with income levels, education, intelligence, bloodlines, race, creed, physical characteristics, or the town we grew up in. Everyone has the raw, untapped ability to create an exciting, balanced, and predictable future in his or her life. Of course, it's convenient to let ourselves off the hook by blaming uncontrollable events and circumstances for our lack of success in life. The only problem is, there are far too many success stories of personal triumph from people who were in the same situation we are. That is, people with less advantage than what you or I have, who have wound up becoming as successful as we all desire to be. In short, there are no excuses.

We've all heard the saying "Successful people do what unsuccessful people choose not to do." It's a clever saying, and while most of us realize it's true, not many of us act upon it. We stay caught in our predictable patterns of performance, unwilling to break our cycle of behavior. Of course, to break the cycle, we have to dig deeper. We have to get down to the root cause of what's stopping us from moving forward. What is it that seems to block us from taking that first step, from trying to achieve success in the first place? What is it that puts the obstacles in our path before we even get started?

The answer is you, me, all of us. Most of us never give ourselves the opportunity to succeed. We continue to get in our own way. Because we're afraid of success, we hide behind mediocrity. Worse, we believe we're not worthy of the abundant blessings that are waiting to be bestowed upon us. We are afraid of failure and success equally. We blame others for our lack of success so readily that it's as if we've been programmed to do this automatically. We never seem to take the responsibility to look at where the real problem lies... within ourselves.

It's like the old story about the woman out walking. She comes across a man down on his knees, under a street lamp. When the woman asks the man what he's doing, he says he's looking for his keys. The kind woman then gets down on her knees to help the man search. After an hour or so of tireless searching, she says, "We've looked everywhere for your keys and haven't found them. Are you sure you lost them here?" The man replies, "No, I lost them in the parking garage, but there's more light out here under the street lamp."

As humans we're not unlike that man searching for his keys. We find it easier to look outside ourselves for the reasons we're not living the life we've always dreamed of. Truth is, we can't look where it's easy or convenient, but rather we must look where it's necessary for us to realize our full potential, however hard that may be. While there are numerous obstacles that will try to stop you along the way to success, the biggest one of them all and the one that will stop you quicker, harder, and longer than all the other obstacles is you. Yes... you!

How many people do you know who have immense ability yet never seem to reach their full potential? Are you one of them? If so, this book will change your life forever.

I urge you to take a moment and evaluate your life. Ask yourself the tough questions. Have you settled for less than you hoped for? Have you compromised more than you should? Have you let opportunities slip by because you feared the change they may bring? Have you smothered any thoughts of striving for greater success out of fear of failure or fear of the hard work it would require? Have you been holding yourself back for so long that you made a habit of mediocrity? Have you forgotten your dream? Or worse, have you forgotten how to dream all together?

If you're like me, you answered yes to some or all of these questions. And if you're like me, there is hope. The dream might have been forgotten but it still lives deep within you. All you have to do is uncover it once more.

Awaken The Dream

> *"Hope is not a dream, but a way of making dreams become reality."*
> — L.J. Cardina Suenens

At the core of your dream is hope. Hope for a better life. Hope for the freedom to choose to live the way you want to live…on your own terms, to the beat of your own drum. When that hope and dream begins to swell up inside of you, when you're starting to hear that voice screaming inside—the one that's telling you you're capable of so much more…that the best is yet to come…then it's time to follow that dream. It's time to act. And you can do it. We all can.

We begin by simply allowing the dream to be. We Dare To Dream. And in doing so we give light to that same hope that has sparked so many other wondrous futures. Look ahead five years and ask yourself, "What would my perfect life look like if I follow my dream?" Then ask yourself an equally important question, "What will it cost me if I don't follow that dream?" The last question is critical because that's the price you pay for shoving your dreams aside and deciding to live life below your potential. Yes, life can be difficult and unfair, but each and every one of us has the opportunity to change. We each have the power to create our own destiny. We simply have to accept the challenge and, in many cases, be willing to open the gifts that are given to us.

Soon after God answered my question with the line from *The Road Less Traveled*, I received another gift. This one was given to me by my daughter, Jami. It was the greatest imaginable gift I could have ever received. It was a gift of health and wealth. It was a gift called USANA.

USANA offered me a clear path to success. It gave me the health products that changed my life, and the distribution channels to help change a multitude of other lives. USANA offered me the possibility to dramatically increase my income. It also gave me the opportunity and support to find the leader within me. It gave me the skills and the business model to be my own boss. To make my own schedule. To succeed beyond my wildest dreams. My personal belief is that USANA can offer you the same opportunities. But whether USANA is your path or not, the fact remains that the opportunity to live your dream is now knocking on your door. You only have to answer. You only have to Dare To Dream.

Think you don't have what it takes? Think you don't have the resources you need? Trust me—everything you need to succeed, you already have. There's nothing mystical to conquer. There's no secret password to get you into the club of the rich and highly successful. More importantly, there are no demons in your closet that can affect you unless you choose to allow them to do so.

Like most people, I once felt unworthy of receiving even the smallest of gifts. It's no wonder we find it so hard to believe success can happen to us. It wasn't enough that I felt undeserving to want more in my life, I struggled just to feel worthy for the meager possessions I already had. What I've learned is that each one of us deserves the best that life has to offer. I cannot state emphatically enough the importance of removing self-defeating beliefs—starting with the delusion that we are not worthy of our dreams. We are! In fact, we always have been. Now, we just need to accept it. *We begin by destroying the perception that we are not worthy of the infinite abundance surrounding us.*

Dare To Dream

> *"Whatever you can do or dream, you can begin it. Boldness has genius, power and magic in it. Begin it now."*
>
> — Goethe

I unequivocally believe that if you're reading this book you're ready for change. You're ready to be accountable and, more importantly, you're ready to dream again. And you will. I promise you that.

It's time to take control of your life. It's time to stand up for what you've always believed in. It's time to let go of your self-limitations and let your dream flourish again. Do you want to continue taking what little is given to you by chance? Or do you want to consciously reach out and grab the wealth and abundance that's out there waiting for you? Do you want to be one of the birds scavenging for scraps from a dirty alley dumpster? Or, do you want to soar over paradise? You deserve success now. We all do. And there's plenty to go around. There's enough abundance for us all…but it's not going to drop itself in our laps. We have to actively pursue it—and that pursuit starts with a dream. And that dream starts with the first step…Daring to Dream.

There is nothing as precious or powerful as someone who has made the decision to start no matter what their circumstances are. Your journey is about to begin. Don't be afraid to begin where you are. You are about to unfurl your wings and soar to new heights and new freedom. The road may seem bumpy and the path may be difficult at times, but I can assure you, when you reach your destination it will all be worth it. With hard work and courage you will find the happiness and satisfaction you've missed for so long. You will find the wealth and success you know deep down you deserve. You will find the empowerment to guide your own life, rather than be guided by forces outside yourself. Most important, you will find that you possess the same beautiful gift all humans are entitled to, but so few accept…the ability to create your own destiny.

All you have to do is Dare To Dream.

At this point, you don't even have to know how or what to dream! We'll cover that in Chapter Two. For now, just Dare To Dream.

In Chapter One, we took the first step committing ourselves to the simple idea that the life we want to live begins the moment we Dare To Dream. And we will dream… later in this chapter. But before we get to this critical step, we must understand why we're dreaming in the first place. After all, what does dreaming have to do with success? Wouldn't we be better off spending our time in the practical pursuit of concrete goals, instead of day dreaming with our heads in the clouds?

Goals are indeed an important part of success. They are like your road map—the markers and milestones that keep you focused on your path, telling you where you're going and how to get there. On the other hand, your dream is the reason you're making the trip. It's your motivation and inspiration. While your goals will certainly give you the measurements to track your progress, and ultimately tell you when you've arrived…it's your dreams that will fuel your progress and make the trip worthwhile. It's your dreams that will give you the passion and determination to overcome obstacles along the way. And it's your dreams that will enrich and fulfill every aspect of your life when you finally accomplish what you've set out to do.

"Nothing happens unless first a dream."

— Carl Sandburg

Chapter Two

Discovering Your Why

What's A "Why?"

"He who has a why to life for can bear almost any how."
— Friedrich Nietzsche

Simply put, your 'why' is your dream…the life you desire to live. It's the reason you seek out success in the first place and the reason you'll leave the safe haven of the status quo, suddenly willing to put your comfort aside and risk failure in its place. When obstacles come up to block you from your success—and they will—your 'why' will give you the fortitude and willpower to overcome and persevere. When you feel like quitting—and you will—your 'why' will give you the energy you need to put one foot in front of the other so you can blast through your own resistance. Ultimately your 'why' is the dream that precedes your goal, and discovering what that is, is one of the most critical steps to success you will ever take.

Remember my afternoon on the balcony of my beach home -- drinking cabernet and watching the birds soar along the waves? That was my "why." Several years before that, I was going nowhere and doing nothing, aimlessly passing time in front of the TV, alone in my apartment, routinely going to a job I didn't particularly like, all while making barely enough money to survive. I was caught in an unconscious circle of despair, one that ended the instant I made a decision to break free from the chains of my routine. In other words, my life changed the moment I Dared to Dream.

In one instant, I forgot about the life I *had* and started to imagine the life I *wanted*. For the first time in years I allowed myself to dream—not the small and safe dreams a woman of my age and means might make, but large, wonderfully impractical and beautiful dreams. I dreamed of having enough money to be independent and the freedom to live my life according to my own rules and not someone else's. I dreamed of traveling around the world, spending time with my children and grandchildren. I dreamed of owning my own home on the beach and, yes, sipping cabernet on the balcony, while feeling the spray of the ocean as it hit my face. I dreamed it all, without limitations or doubt.

Now I realize if anyone had looked at my life in those days they would have laughed. For all practical purposes, I had absolutely no foundation for my dream. There was nothing to indicate that I could accomplish any of it. Nothing in my life suggested I had the ability, education, resources or experience to make any of my dreams come true. And yet, I dreamed anyway, allowing myself to reach for the stars. My dream became my 'why' and the reason I was willing to take the risks I needed to change my life. My dream became the inspiration and fuel that would carry me through every challenge and obstacle I would face. And because of it, a few short years later, I realized my dream, every single bit of it, right down to the soft sand between my toes.

Why was my 'why' so critical to my success? Because without it I would have given up at the first sign of adversity, allowing myself to fall back into old, familiar patterns. Without my "why," every rejection would have been a fatal blow to my journey towards success. But with my 'why' firmly entrenched in my mind, every rejection and obstacle became a challenge. I refused to give up because I knew in my heart exactly why I was doing what I was doing.

Just look at my background. I had no higher education, barely finishing high school. I also came from a dysfunctional family, losing my father when I was only 16, a loss which sent me on a downward spiral that lasted until the age of 50, which is when my life finally began to change. And, let's face it…age 50 isn't normally a time single grandmothers start new careers. I was tired and worn out. I had raised two kids on food stamps and now that they were finally on their own, all I wanted to do was coast to the finish line. I would have been more than content to drift through life, allowing myself to retire to an even blander existence.

If anyone needed a "why," it was me. And thankfully I found it, because that 'why' took me from working 65 hours a week managing a tile and granite showroom to becoming the owner of my own home based business. Today, I'm earning more money than I have in my entire life, and I'm living a life I never thought possible. It wasn't easy, but having my 'why' gave me the strength and motivation to keep moving forward until I succeeded. And believe me, I needed it.

In my business, USANA, I sell amazing wellness products. They change people's lives, but they don't sell themselves. I had to sell them and, unfortunately, I'm someone who hates selling. Not to mention, I hated the idea of being in Network Marketing. Maybe it was my own preconceived attitudes towards Network Marketing, or maybe I feared what other's thought about it. Either way, that negativity created a monumental struggle to take even the tiniest of steps. Whenever it was time to make sales calls, the phone felt like it was 500 pounds. I literally couldn't lift it off the hook. I couldn't even talk to people in person, regardless of how amazing I knew these pharmaceutical grade products were. If my goal had been only to make money selling products, I would have failed. But in addition to my goal, I had my "why." I had my dream. I knew what I was fighting for and I was willing to do whatever it took to make that dream come true.

With that one dramatic shift in attitude, picking up the phone became easy—turning from a dreaded chore into a clear pathway toward the life I wanted to live. Talking to people suddenly became a joy, because not only was I offering them a product that would greatly improve their lives, but I was also inching confidently towards my dream. My new attitude was empowering, giving me the strength to persevere and the desire to continue moving forward.

Truth is, my experience with the 500-pound phone is a small, capsulated version of my entire life. Fear—in all its debilitating forms—was limiting my ability to grow. I had fear of rejection, fear of success, fear of failure, even fear of life. I felt such a profound sense of confusion and lack of clarity that I became paralyzed—unable to take the steps I needed to change my life. Of course, once I had my 'why' crystallized in my head, once I could see it, touch it and, most importantly, articulate it, my life's purpose fell into place. Like someone waving a magic wand over me, I suddenly discovered the key to unlocking my true potential.

Now, I realize your life isn't going to be exactly like

mine. You'll have different fears and roadblocks in front of you than I had, along with different goals and dreams. That's normal. We're all unique. But, what unites us is that we can all confidently and quickly move toward our goals—once we clearly define our "why."

Charting A Course For Your Why

"Reach high, for stars lie hidden in your soul.
Dream deep, for every dream precedes the goal."
— Pamela Vaull Starr

I recently purchased a new car that came with the latest high tech GPS system. I laughed when I first saw it. "Who needs that?" I thought. Well, it turns out *I did*. In fact, I needed it a lot. It's funny, I never realized how often I was lost or heading off-track until I found myself able to chart a course before leaving home. Now even before I pull out of my driveway I know exactly where I'm going, the fastest course to take, and how long it'll take me to get there. It has made me more efficient and punctual. What's more, it has given my driving, oddly enough, a sense of renewed purpose.

The application to our lives is obvious. Just as I would chart a course to get from point A to point B in my car, we need to chart a course for our "why," allowing our personal GPS systems to tell us when we are on or off purpose. Charting a course for our 'why' certainly makes us efficient but, more importantly, it gives our actions strength, aligning our every day activities with our life's purpose.

So, just how do we chart a course for our "why?" Well first, we need to see a clear picture of what we want, where we are going and how we are going to get there. Secondly, we have to be willing to get outside our comfort zone and do things that unsuccessful people choose not to do. We need to think outside the box, reaching a state of consciousness that says, "I will not be denied. I deserve this!" Personally, when I finally reached this state of mind, I began to let go, and in doing so I struggled less. Suddenly my 'why' took over and began to lead me where I needed to go next, showing me the freedom which would ultimately result in the life of excitement, balance and wealth I enjoy today.

All of which leads to an even more important question. "What motivates you?" And just as important, "When was the last time you felt totally aligned and in sync with your life's purpose?"

Discover Your Why
An Exercise for Finding Your Purpose

> *"All acts performed in the world begin in the imagination."*
> — Barbara Grizzuti Harrison

It's time now to Discover Your Why, and because this step is so critical to your future success, I urge you to take your time working through it. You may read this next section in five minutes...but feel free to take hours, days or even weeks to truly Discover Your Why. Be patient with yourself and stay true to your dream. Also, let the exercise unfold in a natural way. Don't rush or settle for the first thoughts that pop into your mind. Rather, dig deep and truly seek to discover what you want in your life. Not what you think you should want or what others say you should want, but what is truly in your heart. *What your higher self wants*! If you truly own your 'why' the universe will align to give it to you. So before you embark on this journey make sure you're working towards the right 'why.' As the old saying goes, "Be careful what you ask for, you just might get it."

The Exercise

Take a few deep breaths. Close your eyes and remember a time in your life when everything seemed carefree, easy and effortless, a time when everything was going your way, when you felt you were in the flow of what I call a *successful vibration*.

Now imagine Five years into the future. If time and money weren't an issue, what would you choose your life to look like? Picture it clearly in your mind's eye. If you could have anything, what would it be?

Now draw an imaginary circle in your mind. Inside that circle is where you are now. It's your comfort zone. It's safe but foggy, uncertain and restrictive. Imagine yourself getting stronger and braver, then see yourself stepping outside of the circle, stepping out of your comfort zone. Imagine the fog is lifting. Your circle is slowly becoming illuminated—turning gold with the light of possibility. Now, expand on the dream you imagined earlier, on your life five years in the future.

What job do you have? What is your boss like? Are you your own boss? How much money do you make? What does your home look like? What kind of car do you drive? Do you travel? How often? Where do you go? How do you feel when you wake up in the morning? When you come home in the evening? What are your passions? Your hobbies? The causes you believe in? How does your family view you? Your friends? Co-workers? Society? What kind of freedom do you have? And most importantly, how does your new life make you feel?

Let your mind wander to a place where anything and everything is possible. Remember, you're imagining what your life would look like if you could have any life you wanted. There are no limitations.

Now take several more deep breaths, then slowly open your eyes and know that you have taken the first major step toward manifesting your dream.

Of course, this exercise is only a starting point. Once you begin to imagine your ideal life you need to write it down. Pin your 'why' to the wall, tape it to your mirror, carry it around in your wallet. Read it out loud every chance you get. Above it all, go through the exercise as many times as you need to, until you can clearly see and articulate what you want your life to be in the future. You'll find new things will come up the more you allow yourself to imagine. As Albert Einstein once said, "Imagination is more important than knowledge," which for those of us who seek to realize our dreams, has never been more true.

Seasoning Your 'why'

> *"An average person with average talent,*
> *ambition and education, can outstrip the most*
> *brilliant genius in our society, if that person has*
> *clear, focused goals."*
> — Brian Tracey

Like many of you, I enjoy the peace and tranquility I feel when I step into a local coffeehouse. I feel instantly relaxed and at peace with the smell of the fresh brewed coffee and hot pastries. The ritual is always the same. I buy my favorite coffee drink then season it with the perfect blend of chocolate, cinnamon, and nutmeg. Although the coffee tastes and smells wonderful alone, adding the seasonings takes it to another level. It makes it custom, personal and, inexplicably, memorable. And, of course, what is true for your coffee is equally true for your 'why.'

You need to imagine your ideal life…then add lots of seasoning. Be specific down to the tiniest details. Yes, you want a job that makes a lot of money, but how much money do you want to make? Put a dollar amount to it. Where is your job? How close to home? Who do your work for or do you work for yourself? How many hours a day? What do you wear? What does your workplace sound like? Smell like? What do you feel like when you're there?

What does your dream home look like? How many rooms do you have? How many bathrooms? What's the color scheme? The layout? The view? What type of fresh flowers do you have in the vase on your kitchen table? What pictures hang in your living home?

You get the idea. Having a general dream isn't enough. It has to be specific. It has to have details. The details are the seasoning to your coffee, enhancing not only your experience but the chances of realizing your dream.

One of the 'whys' I had when I started my journey was a home at the beach. The ocean has always been a place where I could find peace. It grounds me and connects me, allowing me to easily get in touch with my feelings. Of course, in order for my 'why' to become a reality, I had to season it with details, with every possible ingredient I could find. I closed my eyes and visualized the color, size, and layout of my home. I even imagined the seagulls flying over the sandy beaches. I smelled the fresh salt air and listened to the breaking of the waves. Although my beach house was really nothing more than sticks and bricks, when I seasoned my 'why' it provided me with the level of energy to attack the day-to-day challenges that I was being confronted with as I launched my USANA business.

I don't have to tell you I was blessed with realizing my 'why' and finally getting my beach house. It is safe to say that from an emotional standpoint that vision was worth millions to me. In fact it was priceless, teaching me perhaps one my most valuable lessons: the success we achieve in our lives is in direct proportion to how well we can clearly imagine what we want.

The Importance Of Your 'Why'

> *"Hold fast to dreams, for if dreams die, life is a broken-winged bird that cannot fly."*
> — Langston Hughes

I hope that by this point I've communicated the importance of Discovering Your Why. If not, let me be perfectly clear—if you ignore this step—you give up your dream. Certainly, you can look at your 'why' as what you would have in a perfect world, and that's fine. But, to turn your 'why' into something truly powerful, look at it as what you stand to lose. Everyone works harder when they know what they risk losing. And while you can say you can't lose something you don't have, I would argue you already have.

By not living your life to your full potential, by not realizing the dreams you hold so dearly, you have lost what life is offering. Well, now it's time to get your dreams back—only this time, you'll have to fight for them. Of course, by clearly defining your 'why,' you will now know exactly what you're fighting for.

You Are Worthy Of Your 'Why'

> *"You have to believe in happiness, or happiness never comes."*
> —Douglas Malloch

In order to truly live the life you desire, attracting the people and situations into your life that will help you realize your dream, you must first know that you're worthy of receiving all of your dreams and goals. You must be willing to accept happiness. This means taking a close look at what you knowingly and unknowingly hold as true. Your 'why' holds with it the key that will unlock your ability to transcend yourself from mediocrity to greatness. Your 'why' gives you the power to craft a master plan so that you can attract in life what you desire most. But again, if you do not feel worthy, you will block and lockout your ability to create the life you want. If you cannot accept that you deserve abundance, or if you continue to have a negative association with who you are and what you're capable of achieving, then it won't matter how hard you strive. You will find every reason to sabotage and discount each blessing as it comes into your life.

Many of us feel guilty for wanting more. This is self-defeating. We must learn there is no reason to feel ashamed of wanting good thing to come to our lives. We must make the emotional and physical shift to believe we're worthy of all the abundance and wonders we create in our lives. We are all entitled to have abundance in our lives, to radiate prosperity and give back to all those we come in contact with. The past does not equal the future no more than your fears and insecurities define who you are.

You deserve your dream. Everyone does. Trust me on this—you are worthy.

Whys Change

When patterns are broken, new worlds emerge.
— Tuli Kupferberg

You've heard the old saying, "Beauty is in the eyes of the beholder." Well, your 'why' is like beauty itself—it's different for everyone. We each have our own personal, unique key that will unlock our true potential. Your 'why' will obviously be different than my 'why.' Of course, whatever your 'why,' it is my heartfelt desire to help you see how simple it is to create a roadmap for your journey. It is my honor to show you how to move through your resistance to reach your unique destination in life.

Along the way, as you develop and begin enjoying your treasures in life, your 'why' will change and grow with you as well. Because that's a normal part of the process, every once in awhile you should pull out this chapter and go through the exercise of Discovering Your Why again.

But for now, you have your 'why' and are ready to move to the next step towards success—transforming your 'why' from a dream into a vision.

*The moment of
enlightenment
is when a
person's dreams
of possibilities
become images
of probability.*

— Vic Braden

Chapter Three
Declaring Your Vision

While having our 'why' firmly established is a great first step, taken alone it's not enough to guide our journey to success. We have to put our 'why' to work. To paraphrase Vic Braden, we need to turn our dreams of possibilities into images of probability, transforming our 'why' into 'vision' and in the process, taking the first leap toward manifesting the life we dream.

What is Vision?

Restlessness and discontent are the first necessities of progress.
— Thomas Edison

Imagine the thermostat in your home. Get a good, clear picture of it. You probably don't think too much of it during the course of a day, in spite of the amazing role it plays in our lives. Think about it. With the simple push of our finger, a thermostat completely controls our environment, dictating how comfortable or uncomfortable we'll be in our surroundings. If our home is too hot we simply push a lever to the left initiating the electrical currents that signal the air conditioner to turn on a compressor, which begins to chill the air, which is systematically blown throughout the house by a fan. Soon as our environment reaches our desired temperature, the thermostat intelligently shuts the entire system off. And of course, the exact reverse happens with a heater when we want to go from a cold environment to a warm environment. In other words, if we're happy with our environment, we leave our thermostat alone. If we're unhappy with our environment we adjust our thermostat. And perhaps most miraculous of all the thermostat will realize our desires to the exact degree we choose.

For you and I the thermostat is the perfect metaphor for what we hope to achieve with our vision. In fact your vision *is* your thermostat. If you're happy with your life there's no need to adjust it. You're already where you want to be. If, however, you're not happy with your life or you feel you can do much better then you need to adjust your thermostat—fine tuning it until it's exactly where you want to be. This adjustment is tantamount to declaring your vision.

Now, I'm assuming since you're reading this book that you already believe you can achieve a life greater than the one you have now, which means you're probably more than ready to adjust your vision. But before we begin this declaration, it's important to understand the subtle, yet vital distinction between your 'why' and your 'vision.'

Your 'why' is your objective—the temperature you want to reach. On the other hand, your "vision" is taking your dream, objective or 'why' and making it unquestionably real in your mind. Your vision is the commitment and intent behind the 'why' or the force of energy you put into what you want out of life. By clearly declaring your vision—with strength and purpose—you create an ideal in your life that, like the air conditioner or the heater, your mind is obligated to follow. In fact, the more powerful the vision, the more inevitable it will be that your why will be manifested.

You may ask why our minds are obligated to follow our vision. It's a good question and I'll be honest—I don't fully know the answer. What I do know, with every fiber of my being is that it happens whether we understand it or not. The unconscious mind is a wonder of manifestation—naturally and innately producing the energy, motivation, and creative direction we need to achieve our vision. With purity and strength of vision it happens whether we want it to or not. Have you ever wanted to go on vacation and started dreaming of yourself sitting on a tropical beach with an umbrella drink in your hand? What happens? Well, if you imagine that vacation long enough your mind begins to nag at you until soon you find yourself browsing the internet for airfares and hotels. Next, you find yourself talking to family and friends trying to get others involved as well. And, sooner or later you'll probably start saving money or figuring out how to pay for the trip. In short, you start to firmly create your vision (thermostat) and in doing so your unconscious mind (air conditioner/heater) sets in motion a series of actions and events that will help you realize your vision. Maybe it isn't a vacation—maybe it's a job, a relationship, more money—but it's the same principle: your unconscious mind won't rest until the gap between your vision and your reality is completely bridged.

What Does A Vision Do For Us?

The reasonable man adapts himself to the conditions that surround him. The unreasonable man adapts surrounding conditions to himself. All progress depends on the unreasonable man.
— George Bernard Shaw

We all remember the story of *Goldilocks and the Three Bears*. Three Bears live in a small suburb on the city's outskirts. On one bright sunny morning the bears hop a metro bus into the city to do a little shopping at the mall. (Okay, I admit, the story is slightly changed to keep up with the times.) While the Bears are away a young girl named Goldilocks rides up to their house on a moped. She's hungry and tired and is looking for food and rest (her vision.) Normally, she wouldn't break into a house like this, but she's declared her vision and her mind is motivating her to realize it subconsciously sending her the signals she needs to realize it. Once inside she notices the three bowls of porridge. The first bowl is far too hot. The second is too cold. However, the third bowl of cereal is just right. Goldilocks eats the cereal and realizes her vision of finding food to satisfy her hunger.

Making her way to the library Goldilocks noticed three beautifully stuffed chairs. Testing the largest overstuffed chair Goldilocks didn't feel comfortable. The medium-sized, wing-backed chair was not much better. However, the third, smaller chair was just right...until it collapsed. Frightened by the sound of snapping pine Goldilocks quickly ran up the stairs.

The upstairs was a spacious sleeping loft containing three neatly made beds of varying sizes. Goldilocks stretched her small frame on a large bed. It was far too hard to suit her liking. The medium-sized bed was fluffy and soft, but sagged in the middle. The third and smallest bed provided adequate support, was the perfect size, and the bedspread colors matched Goldilocks sundress perfectly. In fact, this bed was just right and Goldilocks fell fast asleep, her dream happily realized.

While the fairy tale is common and simple, the point is profoundly clear. When a strong vision is in place (like Goldilock's vision) people are inherently willing to experiment until they get exactly what they know is right for them. They refuse to settle for less and are committed to breaking through the status quo in their quest to create a new and exciting way of life. With the vision set the mind leads us to where we need to be in our journey and motivates us to take the actions that will help us succeed. Now obviously, we don't want to break the law like Goldilocks did, but the essence of the story remains intact—declare a vision and your mind will set in action the steps you need to take to realize your own vision. Individuals who lack a strong vision or refuse to move outside their comfort zone become so comfortable that they fall asleep, almost in a trance state—trapped by their own contentment.

What this means in our lives is simple. Vision is the catalyst that makes all things in life possible and not just what we see in our minds, but the expectations we have for our lives. It is how we see ourselves, the conversations we have with ourselves, and the way we feel about ourselves in any given situation. *A clear and powerful vision transforms the imaginations in our head into a driving force that compels us to take the necessary steps to ensure that we will become what we were meant to become.* This is the essence of a bold vision—the prerequisite that will allow us to make our dreams a reality.

It has become abundantly clear to me that everyone ends up somewhere in life, however, very few people end up where they wanted to end up—in a place matching their life's purpose. The ones who do are the ones with a vision that will clearly illuminate the road ahead, making their present and future paths clear to see.

What...or Who's...Vision are You Following?

It's what you choose not to see in your life that controls your life.
— Lynn Andrews

Like a thermostat generating cool or warm air, our mind can work in either direction. It can work towards creating a positive vision or a negative vision. We've all heard about the magic of self-fulfilling prophecies—our own internal power to create in our lives exactly what we believe will happen. Studies have proven the reality. In fact, in one particular study a teacher was given different information about the students in her different classes. She was told one class of students was of exceptional intelligence, while the other class of students was simply average. While the truth was that both classes of students were intellectually equal, several months later the students the teacher *thought* were "exceptional" tested far better than the other class of students she *thought* were "average." The class of highly performing students excelled simply because their teacher had a "vision" of that class excelling. She believed in the inevitability of their success. Self-fulfilling prophecies have been proven to work in everything we do. If we believe strongly enough that something will happen, it usually does. At the same time, if we believe something won't happen, that usually manifests itself as well. We all know of someone who was sure they wouldn't get a new job...and didn't. Someone who knew they wouldn't win a game...and didn't. Someone who knew they wouldn't achieve financial independence...and didn't.

All of which brings up a vitally important question— what vision is your mind currently working on? Are you taking control of your visions or allowing them to wander aimlessly on their own—no matter how negative or self-defeating they may be? Have you been so burned by past failures that you believe you will fail at whatever you attempt? Do you believe the success of others limits your own possibility for success? Perhaps, you believe you're not worthy of success? All of these self-defeating beliefs create a vision that is false, predicated on lies and half-truths. And far from being harmless, these passing thoughts become your vision—the steering wheel that guides your journey. Without us even realizing it, these lies become the 'why' our mind is working so diligently to realize. The truth is, the mind doesn't care what it works for—good or bad, truth or lies. In fact, the mind can't even distinguish between reality and imagination, which is why we'll cry, laugh, or wince when we go to the movies. They're not real, but our mind responds to them like they are.

Likewise, your mind doesn't care if your vision is positive or negative either. It only cares that you are realizing the vision you have for yourself. If that vision happens to be negative your mind will happily feed you the action steps you need to accomplish the outcome, however negative it may be. It will even congratulate itself for helping you realize your vision. Mission accomplished. The lesson is obvious. If your mind can't and won't distinguish between what is real and imagined, we need to pay particular attention to what we tell it. This is why our self-defeating thoughts and habits must be eliminated immediately. We need to begin our journey with a clear and well-developed vision.

Of course, even if we don't have negative thoughts of our own, without a clear vision, our mind can still lead us astray by guiding us to realize the vision of others. We already know the mind works towards the vision we feed it. But, if we don't choose that vision consciously, then we choose it unconsciously, or worse, it's chosen for us—often times by those with their own laundry list of self-defeating beliefs. We may be working towards a vision that was programmed in us by our parents, our teachers, society or peer groups. Whether these people had our best interests in mind or not, the point is that if our minds are subconsciously working to realize someone else's vision, then it can't possibly be working towards our own vision of who we want to be.

When you're six months old you obviously don't have strong opinions about who you are as an individual. As babies all we know is we're hungry and we want our diapers changed. And if we don't like what we're fed—we'll spit it out. Life is simple and basic. But as we grow and our lives began to take shape we became more and more influenced by the outside world. Who do our parents want us to be? Our family? Friends? What's the cool way to act and talk in our social cliques? What direction do our teachers want us to take? Without even realizing it, we begin taking on other people's visions, often times forgetting how to instinctively follow our own.

What's so important about understanding the vision building process is that most of these beliefs —who we are and who we want to become—were forced on us because we weren't thinking independently enough to decide whether or not we wanted them in the first place. Of course, it doesn't happen all at once, but incrementally, one unconscious decision at a time.

Now, it's time for us to decide on our own what it is we truly want to believe in, then translate that belief into a vision that will motivate us to achieve the things in life we seek. But before we do that let's expose a few myths about vision so we don't end up going down the wrong road again.

4 Myths About Vision

You can't depend on your eyes when your imagination is out of focus.
— Mark Twain

Myth #1
Your Desire Creates Success

As a society, most of us naively believe that wanting something badly enough will give us the energy to go get it. We buy our lotto ticket and fantasize about the mansion by the ocean and the foreign convertible in the garage. And yet, for as strong as these desires may be, most of us won't achieve any of it. Wealth, financial independence, and even happiness remain elusive dreams seemingly earmarked for the selected few. In fact, a Social Security study conducted by the Bureau of Labor Statistics revealed that from a cross-section of one hundred people at age 65:

- 63% were dependent on Social Security, friends, relatives or charity
- 29% were dead
- 3% were still working
- 4% had accumulated some sort of financial security
- 1% were wealthy

Personally, I believe it's appalling to think we can work 30 to 40 years and then retire on one-half of what we could barely live on for the first 30 to 40 years...and that only five percent of the country will ever figure out how to be financially free, with only one percent ever becoming wealthy.

Since, most of us start off our adult life with the desire to create financial prosperity, it's clear that desire has nothing to do with success. Desire only creates neediness and wanting, the same feelings we get when we step up to buy our lotto ticket. Truth is, desire is a thirst and hunger that will never be satisfied. Most importantly, it won't provide the actual energy we need to stay on course and produce the results we're looking for to help us achieve our goals.

Myth #2
Your Hard Work Creates Success

Ever since we were children we've been told the same thing—"working hard" was the pathway to success and "putting our nose to the grindstone" was the ethic we needed to get ahead in life. And while certainly no one can deny how important good work habits are, their ultimate value is greatly overrated. Face it, we all know the stories—individuals who have worked hard their entire lives, yet still don't have what they want; families who must live on two or three incomes just to get by; men and women who work twelve hours a day, seven days a week, harder than their bosses, only to find at the end of the road they have virtually nothing to show for it.

Working hard will certainly play a major part in your success, but it's a myth to think that working hard alone will produce your desired results, which perhaps is why there is a new mantra for corporate America—"Work smarter, not harder"—a concept we will explore later in the book.

Myth #3
Your Ability To Be A Good Person Creates Success

Be the best person you can possibly be. You can't argue with that. In fact, I believe there's no greater ideal an individual can aspire to than this. But what does being a good person have to do with success? Unfortunately, very little. While nice guys may not always finish last, they don't always finish first either. After all, how many successful jerks do you know? Truth is, money has no conscience. It simply doesn't care where it goes. History is littered with healthy, happy, and wise individuals who have led simple, impoverished lives. Now, even if they lived these lives by choice it's proof enough that being a good person alone won't bring you success...not the monetary kind. Of course, I'm not saying that monetary success should be your only goal. It absolutely shouldn't be. But, neither should the pursuit of material wealth be vilified. It's a worthy pursuit and for the purposes of this book, a main focus of our journey. Like hard work it's a desirable trait and one that may contribute to your success and happiness, but it's imperative to shatter the myth that being a good person alone will bring you success. If that were true, we'd see a lot more independently wealthy four year olds.

Myth #4
Your Level of Education Creates Success

This is a tough one for us to understand. While education supports us in our growth and will undoubtedly give us many of the tools we need to succeed, education alone isn't the path to success. Again, you probably know too many well-educated people who aren't particularly successful, just as you may know some high-school drop-outs who are wealthy beyond measure. Take your education seriously, whether you get it in schools or in the real world...just don't allow yourself to fall into a false sense of security believing that education alone is going to give you everything you need to succeed.

It's clear that all four statements contain elements of truth in the pursuit of success. Where they become myths, however, is in believing that these elements alone are all we need to succeed.

So if desire, hard work, being a good person, and education isn't the key to success—what is?

Vision Produces Motivation...Motivation Produces Action

Take away the cause, and the effect ceases.
— Miguel de Cervantes

Let me make this perfectly clear: motivation is at the heart of all genuine and lasting achievement. Success is and always will be determined by how motivated a person is, which will be directly determined by the strength of one's vision. In fact, the degree to which a person has the powerful motivation to pursue his or her dreams is the degree to which he or she will move through the obstacles that would easily defeat others. Face it, the path between where we are today and where we want to be ten years down the road is filled with challenges and adversity. The difference between the person who succeeds and the person who doesn't is a matter of horsepower—our internal motivation to keep going in spite of the obstacles we face. If your vision is powerful enough it will fortify you with the energy, stamina, and the ability to continue on when others would fall prey to failure and defeat.

Interestingly enough most people who fail don't realize there's very little difference between them and the people who succeed in achieving their dreams. What's the difference between a major league hitter with a .300 batting average and one who has a .200 batting average? About $3 million dollars a year! And what makes that difference? One hit. One base hit more out of ten and you're a superstar. Truth is, the difference between success and failure in all our lives is a matter of inches and fractions or, more accurately, our willingness to take that one extra step when the person next to you has just quit. This determination is fueled only when we have the proper motivation, for with motivation comes physical energy. It seems the people who are powerfully motivated always seem to have the energy to do what needs to be done. They have the creativity to find solutions to their challenges and the courage to push outside their comfort zone. On the other hand, people who aren't properly motivated lack this energy along with the creativity and courage to realize their dreams.

So how can we know whether or not we are properly motivated? You need to look at your actions. If your actions are in alignment with you dreams and inspirations then you're motivated. If you're not in action and are not progressing towards your dreams and inspirations you're not motivated. It's as simple as that. You either have it or you don't.

Of course, the question naturally arises—how do you get motivated if you're not currently moving in alignment with your dreams? If there is one secret to my success in network marketing (and any business for that matter), it's the ability to be self-motivated in the continuous development of my vision, while simultaneously pursuing my purpose in life. For me, constructively developing the vision sets the thermostat of my mind to the environment I want, and in doing so, my mind automatically sets in motion the guidance, direction and actions I need to accomplish that vision. And most importantly, my mind gives me my motivation, which equals energy, desire and persistence. With that I can accomplish anything. So can you.

Developing Your Vision

Man is made by his belief. As he believes, so he is.
— Bhagavad-Gita

So now we come to the heart of it. We know what vision is, what it isn't, why we need it, and how it can helps us. But how do we develop our vision?

First off you already have a vision. Everyone does. It's not a matter of getting a vision, it's a matter of replacing the one you have with a new one that propels you towards the things in life you desire most. Because you defined your 'why' in Chapter Two, you already know what you want. To develop your 'why' into a vision all you need to do is own it on a deep and personal level. It's not enough to say you want something, you have to believe it to the core of your being. *You have to live as if you already have it.*

Remember what we said about the mind earlier? It can't tell the difference between reality and imagination. It will work equally hard on either behalf. So in developing your vision you need to imagine your 'why' as if you already have it. Treat is not as something you'll have at some distant point in the future, but as something you already have now. It might sound crazy and counter intuitive, but if you take a leap of faith and embrace this simple technique everything in your life will begin to shift. The people you interact with, the situations you encounter, the challenges presented to you—they will all adapt and change to facilitate the realization of your vision. It won't work by just desiring your "why,"—you have to honestly and truly believe with every fiber of your being that you already have it. You have to transform it into a vision.

Next, to reinforce your belief in your vision, you can give yourself tools to help you along. Write yourself notes and affirmations that declare your vision in the present tense.

I am a millionaire.
I am independently wealthy.
I am a successful entrepreneur.
I live the life I have chosen for myself.

Create a list of your own present tense affirmations, then picture those affirmations in your mind. Visualize them every day and several times a day. Put clear pictures of your vision in your mind and let your mind go to work on it. Draw pictures or clip pictures from magazines that represent your vision, then imagine yourself in those same pictures. Most of all, believe in the reality of your vision.

Remember, vision is our thermometer. It's the expectation that sets motivation into action. Desire alone isn't enough. Making the list of your 'whys' isn't enough. You have to own it, believe it, live it. You have to EXPECT IT!

Finally, trust yourself to know that once you declare your

vision it's already done. I can't emphasize this enough. There is no single greater action you can take on the path to success than declaring and embracing your vision. A well defined vision gives you the passion, motivation, direction, and purpose to jumpstart your daily production and move confidently towards the realization of your dreams.

I am more afraid of an army of 100 sheep led by a lion than an army of 100 lions led by a sheep.

— Talleyrand

Chapter Four
Defining Your Leadership Role

It doesn't matter whether you run a country, a Fortune 500 company or a troop of Cub Scouts, you need to know how to lead if you and your organization are going to be successful. Our ability to lead is the ultimate differentiator between success and failure, wealth and poverty. A great leader will inspire an organization to tap into their true potential, helping them excel far beyond their wildest imaginations, while a poor leader will inevitably prevent the organization from reaching even the tiniest fraction of their potential. As your journey towards success begins you must realize that you can't merely be a follower if you're going to get where you want to go. To truly realize your vision, you need to lead—with passion, commitment, and purpose. You need to ask not if you will be a leader, but how great a leader are you willing to become. Your answer will determine your future.

Let me go on the record right now and say I believe leadership is inherent in all people. It only needs to be discovered, developed, and fine-tuned. If you have the desire and courage to lead, you can lead. It's as simple as that. Of course, there are skills and qualities you will need to develop, but they are easily and readily accessible to anyone who has the patience and determination to incorporate them into his or her life. Because you're already reading this book, I can assume you're undoubtedly ready to learn, ready to take that first step toward leadership greatness. So let's begin.

True Leaders Lead Themselves

> *Too many people overvalue what they are not and undervalue what they are.*
> — Malcolm Forbes

If we ask why people choose to follow instead of lead, we must also ask why people choose mediocrity over greatness, a life of "status quo" over one of purpose and challenge. In other words, why aren't there more leaders in the world? The answer, of course, is as close as the mirror. What prevents people from leading is an inability to look at one's self and say "I want to take you to a better place." Put another way, we don't lead because of our unwillingness to lead ourselves. Yes, it's true—in order to lead you need people to follow. But more than that, you need complete mastery over your own life. After all, if you can't manage your own life, how can you manage anyone else's? If you can't inspire yourself to achieve, how can you inspire others? If you can't realize your own potential, how can you ask someone else to realize his or her own?

Face it, people instinctively know when a leader is worth following. They may not understand the reason, but it doesn't matter. It's human nature. We are all inexplicably drawn to individuals who we know can take us to where we need to go. We not only admire, but gravitate to those individuals who have the courage and persistence to realize their own potential—individuals who have dedicated themselves to the simple proposition that we have a sacred duty and responsibility to become all that we are capable of becoming. These are individuals who *live the same truths and ideals* they demand of those in their own organization. These are individuals who have begun their journey the only place you really can begin—with themselves. To be truly successful and achieve the dreams you want, you must become this individual. And, as is the law of the universe, once you do—once you become what you know you are capable of becoming—others will flock to your presence. They will seek out your leadership and allow you to inspire them to greatness.

Of course, to become this person you must start with an honest evaluation of yourself. This means examining exactly where you're coming from. What are your motives? Your intentions? Are you a person of your word? Do you make clear and effective plans, then follow through on them? Are you committed? Dedicated? Passionate? Courageous? Just asking these questions will start the process. You see, as you begin to examine your own life and your mastery of leadership qualities, you will naturally begin to align your actions with the characteristics you need to lead. As explained in the last chapter, your mind will want to fill the gap between where you want to be and where you are now. But again, this process can only begin with an honest self-evaluation followed by a clear commitment to developing the qualities you need to lead.

Communication

Outstanding leaders appeal to the hearts of their followers - not their minds.
— Unknown

Selling your vision isn't just a matter of telling it to your team, but of connecting it to the organization you want to lead. This connection is the key to communication—a process that involves both speaking and listening, giving and taking. Meaningful communication is a two-way street. Ideas and feedback need to flow back and forth between you and the people on your team so the vision becomes not yours or theirs, but the entire team's. This is how you will create ownership, buy-in, enthusiasm, passion and persistence—the essential ingredients for success.

From a childhood fight on the playground to a world war and everything in between, most of the problems in our society come from a failure to communicate—a failure to say what we mean and mean what we say. As leaders, there is so much out of your hands, so many things you can't control, that you should take every opportunity to seize and master the things you *can* control. This begins with your voice. We each need to strive to communicate with 100% in the moment awareness. We need to choose the right message for the right individual, and more importantly, infuse that message with passion and honesty. Remember, your organization will follow you only to the degree to which they believe in *you*—and not just your *words*. Our words must be empowered by both the message and the conviction that stands behind it. It will always be the intent behind our words that the listener hears. In other words, believe in what you're saying. Nothing will shoot your credibility down faster than insincerity. And once you've lost credibility, you've lost the ability to effectively lead. On the other hand, communicate simply and clearly—with passion, honesty and sincerity—and people will follow you anywhere.

Bottom line: you need to communicate. You can't afford not to. And contrary to popular belief, communication doesn't begin with speaking but with listening. Listening is always the first step to effective communication. In fact, without listening there can be no real and meaningful communication.

You need to listen to every single man and woman in your organization. You need to find out what drives them to get up in the morning. What can you do to help them succeed and provide for their families? How do they feel about their teammates? The role they play in the organization? Are they empowered? Inspired? Bored? Fed up? Do they feel they can make a difference in your team's future? The degree to which you listen to them and completely understand your team members is the degree to which you can help them succeed. And as is the reciprocal nature of life, the more you help them, the more they will help you. It's not just good business practice, it's good people practice.

Character And Ethics

> *Nearly all men can stand adversity, but if you want*
> *to test a man's character, give him power.*
> — Abraham Lincoln

As mentioned earlier, to become a leader you need to find your inspiration in the only place you can—within yourself. The ability to lead effectively depends on where your voice is coming from. Do you find yourself living the truths others believe or what others would want you to believe—or do your words and actions resonate with the truth that comes from a life of *authenticity and integrity*? While character and ethics are many things—honesty, obligation, duty and morality—it is this *authenticity* and *integrity* that is the true hallmark of a character-driven life. It is what truly defines us.

Robert Louis Stevenson said, "That to be who we are and to be what we're capable of becoming is the only end in life." To thine own self be true. Authenticity is the path to being yourself. It means not letting the job, title, money, power, difficulties, challenges or any other outside influences turn you into something you're not. Authenticity is the harmony that comes when what you say, think, and do coincide with what you believe. To be authentic is to communicate with honesty, warmth, humor, and sincerity.

Integrity is the simple act of doing what's right when no one else is watching. It's not something you can see, but a code of behavior that we choose to live by for the basic reason that it's who we are. It asks you not to just say your words, but live by them—to say what you mean and mean what you say. Integrity is our principles—our commitment to the group as well as to the goals we hope to achieve. Sophocles once said he'd "rather fail with honor than succeed by fraud." To be a leader, you must first speak truth, then stand behind your words no matter the cost.

Be authentic and have integrity and you will be inspirational. Be inspirational and you'll be a leader others will not only respect, but will want to follow.

Expect The Best in People

The art of being wise is knowing what to overlook.
— William James

On the surface, the challenge of a leader is simple: field the most talented team you can find and inspire them to do their best. In reality, your job as a leader is more complex than this. Your job is not just to recognize and inspire talent, but to also put the best talent in the right positions. This means focusing not on your teams' weaknesses, but on their strengths. After all, everyone has weaknesses, which doesn't necessarily mean they or your team are doomed to failure. The key to success is developing your team members' strengths then leading them accordingly.

Through one-on-one discussions, observation, and trial and error, you will begin to recognize what the right job for the right person is. You will learn and develop the skill of recognizing the individuality of everyone on your team. This skill starts by accepting the obvious: we're not all created equal. Our talents and skills are as varied as our personalities. Some of us are better at numbers, others are better with people; some of us are strategists, while others are motivators, salesmen, enforcers, or mediators.

What's more, many individuals might not even know their own strengths and talents. That's where you come in. As a wise and observant leader, you will see what others can't see, and recognize talent where others don't. This takes fresh eyes and an open mind.

Leader's often think it's enough to tell their team, "Look, it's your job, I've shown you how to do it…now do it." While on paper that might make sense, reality is very different. Leading a team is like doing a puzzle—trying out people at different tasks, putting them in different situations and with different people, searching for that "exact fit" where they can stand out and flourish.

As leaders, it's your job to help your people find purpose, meaning and value in their jobs. In the same way you can't fit a square peg through a round hole, you can't fit the right person into the wrong job—unless you're willing to settle for mediocrity. On the other hand, the more you put the right person in the right slot, the more powerful you make the individual…and your team.

I believe in expecting the best in all people. It's a self-fulfilling prophecy that works as well with the individuals in our team as it does with the visions we want to create in our lives. But to expect the best in others you have to meet them where they are. It's a worthless effort to attempt to make people into something they're not.

And in the same way people have different strengths and weaknesses, people are also motivated by different things. Some are motivated by pain and struggle, others by pleasure and an eye on the prize. Some are competitive, others aren't. It's up to you to identify the appropriate motivation that will move your team forward. Remember, most people will do more for someone else than for themselves, so you can trust that they'll come through for your team as long as you bring out the best they have to offer.

Recognition

A man doesn't live by bread alone. He needs buttering up once in a while.
— Robert H. Henry

People will go to the ends of the earth for recognition. Yes, we all want money and titles, but deep down we want to be valued and respected, which means being recognized for the efforts we make and the accomplishments we achieve.

It's such a simple concept, but one that many leaders

overlook. Maybe leaders are afraid of letting their team get too overconfident. Maybe they think their team won't work as hard if they're contented with praise. And perhaps still others think that being paid to do your job is enough reward on its own. Whatever the case, a good leader must realize that recognition is a vital part of managing any organization. In fact, it's essential to taking your team to the next level.

Typically, people have no problems pointing out weaknesses in others, and in many cases, this can be a critical step towards success as well. Unfortunately, one of the biggest complaints workers have today is that their leaders only see the negative in what they do—or at the very least, it's what they focus on most. As leaders we need to focus on what our team is doing right. This not only sends a message that we value *results*, but the *individuals* that produce those results. Just as important, it empowers our team to work harder and achieve even greater results. Recognize individuals, recognize your team, and don't forget to recognize yourself as well!

Be Passionate

Nothing great in the world has been accomplished without passion.
— George Hegel

Behind every great artistic masterpiece and every significant work of literature and music there has always been passion. Behind every innovative company, every earth shattering idea and every achievement that ever changed the world, there has always been passion. In fact, behind every dream that ever saw its way out of the imagination and into reality, there has always been passion. And, of course, behind every future success you hope to achieve, there must also be passion. It is not a luxury, but rather a mandate for achieving our dreams.

Simply put, passion is that burning fire in our belly that compels us to do more than we ever thought possible. To be passionate is to be enthusiastic, inspired and motivated for the simple reason that you love what you do. And what happens when you love what you do? The same thing that happens when you fall in love: the world changes. When you love what you do, you not only do it more often, but also better, with more intensity, drive and purpose. This not only adds meaning and joy to your lives, but productivity to your work.

Without a doubt, passion is the great transformer in our organizations. Its power belongs to us all, not just to rock stars, astronauts, firemen or CEOs featured in the Wall Street Journal, but to anyone who chooses to live a life of purpose. Passion is the fuel to every one of your dreams. It is what will create the miracles in your life.

As a leader you'll quickly find that you get what you attract in life, and if you're passionate about your work you'll attract passionate people. It's a simple law of nature: passion is contagious...and it only takes one individual to get the ball rolling. That individual is the leader—and that leader is *you*.

Commitment

Unless you are willing to drench yourself in your work beyond the capacity of the average man, you are just not cut out for positions at the top.
— J.C. Penny

Most people don't follow uncommitted leaders. Your team has to know that not only are you in this for the long haul, but that you're committed to winning—making the sacrifices you need to make for the good of the team. When push comes to shove and you're down to crunch time, most people will inevitably band together to accomplish what needs to be accomplished. Of course, they'll do it only if their leader is willing to go the extra mile with them—to boldly lead the way. Commitment is more than getting the job done; it's getting the job done with excellence. This takes focus and determination.

If you're not in the game or distracted, your team—sensing your lack of commitment—will fall apart when you need them most. Of course, there will obviously be times when you are distracted or not fully attentive to your team. It's human nature. During these times, it's critical not to let your team recognize this. Do what you need to do to get back on track immediately. Figure out why you're distracted. Do you need a new goal? Do you need to reset your expectations? Get your energy back? Redefine your vision statement? Whatever the case, you need to sort it out and get yourself back in the game as quickly as possible. Vincent Van Gogh once said, "I am seeking. I am striving. I am in it with all my heart." Commitment is your ability to not just be in the game, but in the game with all your heart. Do that and your team will follow you anywhere.

Accountability

A leader is one who knows the way, goes the way and shows the way.
— John C. Maxwell

By this time, you can probably define the leader's accountability by yourself. Do what you say and say what you do. Talk the talk and walk the walk. Accountability calls us to be true to our word, both to ourselves and to our team. This is simple, common sense. It might take some practice, and it's certainly something you can continue to work on until you become accountable not just for large commitments, but even for the smallest, most insignificant promises.

Of course, as much as we need to hold ourselves accountable, we must hold our team accountable for their words and actions as well. If we hold them accountable with clear expectations, our people will realize we trust them and genuinely believe in their abilities. By making accountability an absolute requirement, we not only create individuals with a vested interest in their outcome, but also go a long way in creating a culture of leadership, the basic premise that we are all leaders. We might not all be in positions of leadership, managing people and dictating policies, but we can all clearly influence others, and implement positive action and effect change. We can all make a difference and, in doing so, we can all become leaders.

Also, as much as we hold our team accountable for their words, we must hold them accountable for their attitudes. It's easy for a leader to get caught up in the role of a co-dependent, buying into a team member's negativity. You care for your team and you want them to do well. So when they have a problem you naturally want to help them through it. And while it's good leadership to respond to a team member's crisis, you have to make sure you don't spend more time being a counselor than a contributor to the success of the team. While people will always complain and we must certainly permit them to voice their concerns, we must enable them to do it in a platform that allows them to move forward. Otherwise, they'll suck you dry, drain your energy, and if you let them, drag you right down into the abyss of negativity with them.

So listen to the blaming, complaining, and excuses—then direct your team in a way that gets them back on track. Guide them to refocus on what's important to them and the organization. We can turn the situation from negative to positive by holding them accountable for their commitments no matter how many excuses they have to offer.

While you might occasionally feel like the bad guy, even viewed as uncompassionate by some, ultimately your team will see you for who you are—a leader who is as committed to their success as they are—maybe even more so. And they will respect and thank you for not only letting them voice their negative issues, but for helping them move through their negativity and back to the positive accountability they need to succeed.

Courage

> *Greatness lies not in being strong, but in the right use of strength.*
> — Henry Ward Beecher

As a leader you may have the ability, intellect and wisdom to know what needs to be done to drive your team forward, but it's only with courage that you are able to act.

Who are the people we admire most? The people who stand for something when it's not easy or popular. People who will do things nobody else wants to do. People who will speak their mind when no one else will. People who will act from a sense of purpose when others are acting from their own self-interest. In short, people who act from the simple premise that we should "say and do" only that which is "right and true." In an ideal world these people are our leaders. These people are you.

We all have our Achilles heel, an area in our life where we feel lacking and vulnerable. Our choice is simple: we can avoid it or deal with it head-on. As the often-quoted Mark Twain said, "Courage isn't the absence of fear, it's the mastery of fear." Whether it's being afraid to speak in public, having to fire somebody, share an alternative viewpoint or simply telling someone when they're not doing a good job, as a leader you must do what is right for the team. Even when it's hard. And even more so, when it's unpopular.

If every day you were to do one thing that you were afraid to do—but know needs to be done—you could transform your team in a month. Try it. You'll surprise yourself.

From grade school to the Fortune 500, peer pressure still hits us where it hurts—the ego. Whatever age we are, nobody wants to be derided, scorned or ostracized. Nobody wants to be disliked or on the outside looking in. Unfortunately, that sometimes comes with the leader's job. Your job is not to be loved, but respected. And ultimately, you must make your decisions based on what is best for the team as a whole.

As a leader your real power doesn't come with grand and monumental acts, but with the small courage of every day life. The courage that comes with every choice you make: to treat people fairly when no one is watching, to keep trying when you don't immediately succeed, to go the extra mile when nobody asks you to, to take risks and make sacrifices. Nobody sees this type of courage, but it defines you. You can't expect to be courageous when everything is on the line, unless you cultivate the spirit of courage in your every day life.

Let Others Lead

> *Empowerment is all about letting go so that others can get going.*
> — Kenneth Blanchard

Leaders can easily fall into the trap of always wanting to be front and center. After all, leadership is power and power is seductive, the ultimate aphrodisiac. Truth is, it's artificial power. In the long run it doesn't really work. The best leaders are the ones who can step back and encourage others to lead. Making yourself indispensable as a leader might be good for your ego, but it's bad for your team…and your path to success. If you have to be present at every meeting, every event…how much flexibility do you have to truly lead? If you have to make every decision and approve every process, you'll find yourself a slave to forces you can't control, your schedule and attention continually dictated by others. It leaves you little, if no time to lead.

Leaders need to create an environment where mutual trust is fostered—one in which the leader will want to share his burden with those around him, and in return, those around him will feel as if their contributions are encouraged, valued and needed. Empowering the individuals in your team with responsibility, accountability, and autonomy will not only offer the leader lasting support but will strengthen the entire workforce. It is like a chain-reaction: responsibility leads to initiative and initiative leads to an increase in confidence, which leads to self-respect, pride, and ultimately ownership of your business. And what more can a leader want than to have the individuals in his or her organization feel as if they own the place where they work?

True leadership will always be about letting other people shine. As long as you are the center of all things you leave your team in your shadow. Only when you step out of the way and let others rise, will you create new leaders who will duplicate your efforts rather than overwhelm you with theirs. Create leaders and you will become free to lead your team to greatness.

You've Dared to Dream. You've found your 'why.' You've declared your vision. You've defined what it is to be a leader. Your car is revved up and you're approaching the starting line. Now it's time for the race to begin.

The accomplishment of your dreams and goals will be in direct proportion to the financial vehicle you use to drive through life.

— Christian D. Warren

Chapter Five

Driving the Right Vehicle

The Driver's Formula for Success

We've clearly established that we need a vision to realize our dreams—a clear image of what we want to achieve in our lives. And yet, that's still not enough. History is littered with men and women who have lived and died with bold, unrealized ambitions left in their imaginations. While our dreams must certainly take root with vision, they cannot flourish without purposeful action. And more than action, they need a plan or system of behavior—a repeatable formula that works equally for anyone with the perseverance to follow it. That is the key to wealth and success. The key to all of our dreams.

As a collective country, we have always struggled with the issues of making an income…and not just supporting our families, but finding enough wealth to sustain the lives we truly want to live. We sit with our families around the kitchen table, we gather in cubicles with colleagues or in pubs with our friends, all looking for the next big idea—the answer to that age old question: "How can I make a buck?" And, more importantly, "How can I make big bucks, the kind of meaningful, life-changing income that will allow me to work less and, if I'm lucky, not work at all?"

Most of us scratch our head at the questions, inwardly laughing at the improbability of it all, then invariably resign ourselves to our nine-to-five jobs, weekly lotto tickets and our Walter Mitty like fantasies we secretly know will never materialize. We tell ourselves we can't do it; that dreams— the big ones anyway—are for the other guy. We tell ourselves we don't have the time. The money. The know-how. The opportunity. We tell ourselves all sorts of half-truths, and then slowly, over years, convince ourselves that this is reality.

Well, I'm here to unequivocally say that nothing could be further from the truth. The answer to our financial freedom is right in front of our noses. It doesn't matter what we have or where we come from. If we have the vision, the passion and the sincere desire to work hard, our financial situations can change dramatically within a matter of a few short weeks, even days. It doesn't take a lot of time. And you don't need boatloads of money. Whether you want to work full-time or part-time, work for twenty years or retire in three, the access to your dreams is waiting for you. And all it begins with a plan, a formula for success. I call it the **Driver's Formula for Success**. Commit to following it and you will see for yourself just how far you can go and how much you can accomplish with your life.

The Power of the Formula

I learned a long time ago that the secret to creating wealth is in doing the right things consistently and long enough in order to achieve your desired results. I realized that no matter how big your dreams or goals are, the financial formula you "choose to use" will directly affect whether or not you achieve your desired results. In short, we need the right formula. Unfortunately, most of us are using a formula that is outdated and useless, one that does not inherently contain the mechanics of wealth. And because of this, the cards are stacked against us. No matter how vivid our dream is, no matter how hard we work and persevere, we will never get to our desired level of success unless we change the formula we're using, unless we change the financial vehicle we use to drive through life.

At first glance the word formula seems simplistic, robotic, and almost too easy. On second glance you'd be right. It is simplistic, robotic and easy. That's also what makes it work. A formula can be defined as a "more or less invariable way of doing something to achieve a particular end." In other words, if you follow the plan you'll get the results. Isn't that what we all want? Results? It's certainly why our bookstores are lined with self-help books and motivational tapes. We're all looking for results. A plan to call our own. A formula we can trust. Ultimately, the challenge lies not in whether we use a formula or not, but in finding the right formula…one that works to help us achieve the goals we seek in life.

The Right Formula

The formula I'm about to share with you has proven itself to be a powerful avenue to success, one that will unquestionably produce results for anyone willing to follow it. For the purpose of this book, I am referring to the particular formula that will bring both independence and financial freedom to the home based business.

I believe every formula must have six essential pre-requisites for it be a successful and effective means for helping us achieve our goals:

1. *The right formula must work for everybody.* It must be understood and equally applicable for the average hardworking person. The right formula is non-discriminatory. It has no age or education requirements. The right formula should also allow anyone with a work ethic to get in business with a low start up cost. Success is not and never should be the sole domain of the rich.

2. *The right formula must produce a repeatable system in which the individual can "duplicate him or herself" many times over.* As you will soon see, even if you choose not to work, your income should not only survive, but thrive.

3. *The right formula must offer the individual the opportunity to work from anywhere.* Financial and personal freedom means there should be no chains, restrictions, or standards about what work should look like. You can work at home or work in an office. It's your choice. The flexibility of hours is also yours and accordingly, so is the amount of money you can earn.

4. *The right formula must allow the average person the necessary time to learn how to change their values, shifting from an employee mentality to one of independence and self-reliance.* The right formula teaches us how to harness the power that will put us back in the financial driver's seat.

5. *The right formula must offer the luxury of putting your business on autopilot, allowing the money to*

keep flowing month after month.

6. *The right formula must allow your business to withstand any adversity and challenges that may come along.* The right formula will never be built on sand, allowed to wash away with the first high tide; rather it will be built out of steel with proven, concrete principles that work.

And where is that right formula? It's here. Right in front our noses. It is the **Driver's Formula for Success**. It supports any individual who wants financial independence, and who truly wants to learn the secrets to building businesses, which are not only highly equitable, but more importantly, transferable—something you can pass on to your children when you retire. After all, if you're going to be spending your days working hard, you should be creating something that will be yours forever.

The Driver's Formula for Success

> *There is only one success—to be able to spend your life in your own way.*
> — Christopher Morley

The Driver's Mindset

There are two types of people in this world—those who make it happen and those who talk about making it happen. Those who "do it" and those who give excuses for "not doing it." Invariably, the excuse makers are from your typical "employed" mentality, while the make-it happen-folks are from the "business building-investor type" mentality—individuals who are simply looking for a formula that contains the mechanics of wealth, one that will allow them enough transitional time to make the mental, emotional, and physical changes necessary to succeed. These individuals understand the value of a team and have a clear understanding that the individual can't do it alone. They realize the power of the "right formula" to support them in every aspect of their business, virtually guaranteeing that if they remain motivated, hard working, and committed to the formula—they cannot help but succeed. They realize that while it may take time, their results are in their own hands, believing in the simple law of nature that says: *right and consistent effort will always produce desired results.*

A Word of Advice Before We Begin: Follow the Recipe

As we get ready to embark on this new phase of our journey, we should remember that our formula for success is like a puzzle—every piece is important to get the full effect. No one piece is more important than the other. In fact, think of the formula as a recipe for success. When you follow the recipe exactly, you get the exact results you want to achieve—wealth, freedom and prosperity. If you don't follow the recipe you don't get the results. It's as simple as that.

When I grew up my mom made some of the best Tollhouse cookies in the world. I thought she was just a brilliant cook until one day I learned her secret. She had a recipe on the back of the package. She followed the recipe to the letter, step-by-step, and always the same. And because of this, every time her cookies came out just as perfect as the previous time. She never deviated. I quickly realized you didn't have to be a nuclear physicist or Julia Childs to get the results my mom was getting. All you had to do was follow the timeless, proven recipe and anyone could get the same perfectly golden chocolate chip cookies. It was the repeatable system that brought my mom success. Of course, if she had chosen to wing it and experiment with all sorts of deviations, maybe she would have gotten a good cookie and maybe she wouldn't have. It would have been a matter of trial and error.

Now I can't speak for everyone, but I got tired of trial and error a long time ago. I decided I wanted the exact results I wanted to achieve and nothing less. In fact, I refused to settle for less. And guess what? I didn't have to. All I needed was the right recipe and the patience and strength to follow it to the letter.

That's what I'm giving you today—the perfect recipe. The perfect formula for success. Follow it confidently in order to achieve the results you desire.

The Five Essential Keys

> Every man is the architect of his own fortune.
> — *Sallust*

Getting from point A to point B is a concept we can all understand. We want to get somewhere and we have to figure out how to get there. What route do we want to take? What car? How much gas will we need? What will the driving conditions be like? It is not only the perfect analogy for those of us who seek our financial independence, but the conceptual cornerstone for the **Driver's Formula for Success**.

Let's get right to the recipe. There are five essential keys every driver must have in order to reach his or her financial destination. They are:

1. Start With The Right Financial Vehicle.
2. Learn To Drive.
3. Put The Right Gas Into The Vehicle.
4. Go Back To School.
5. Find New Drivers.

Step 1: Start with the Right Financial Vehicle

All the formulas and systems in the world would mean nothing if they don't start with the right ingredients…the right vehicle. The most talented NASCAR driver can be reduced to humiliating failure with a poorly serviced car, as would the virtuoso violinist forced to play a grossly out-of-tune instrument. Talent and skill mean nothing if you don't start with the right equipment. The same is true in our struggle for meaningful income. We each need to start with the right financial vehicle—one that will take us from the "A of our dreams" to the "Z of their realization." Stopping at H or M or even Y is unacceptable. We need a vehicle that will take us all the way to complete and unequivocal financial freedom.

Of course, there are many financial vehicles to choose from—we can be attorneys, doctors, accountants, teachers, writers, hair stylists, bankers, and mechanics. The list is endless, each vehicle with its own value and contributions to our society. And, believe me, the last thing I want to do is detract you from pursuing a genuine calling you may feel in your heart. If you're drawn to a particular vehicle or profession, by all means, jump in and go for it with all you've got. On the other hand, if you're looking to support that profession or to find something altogether more lucrative... read on. I suspect if you picked up this book in the first place, you will probably fall into the latter.

Before we go further, I think it's probably a good time to step back and take another look at exactly what we want out of life. Now your knee-jerk response might be to say you want a new Mercedes-Benz, a fancy house in the Hamptons, or a cruise around the world. Dig a little deeper and you might thoughtfully say you want to provide a college education for your children or a comfortable retirement for yourself and your spouse. Dig even deeper and you'd probably get to an even more profound truth—you want to spend your days doing what you love to do, whatever that may be: teaching, building homes, mentoring, writing, painting, loafing, vacationing, visiting friends or enjoying the sunset.

Let's face it, life is short and we should all spend our days doing what brings us the most joy and purpose. In fact, that's what this book is about—having it all. We should be able to provide for our families and our future, while driving that Mercedes-Benz and spending our days at the beach. Is it a challenge? Yes. Is it doable? Absolutely. All it takes is balance, which simply requires that we work smarter, not harder.

Unfortunately, the existing paradigm of our society says we can't do this. We can't have it all. We are conditioned from an early age to believe that in order to earn more, we need to work more. And if we work more, our leisure time becomes less. Conversely, the other side of this faulty paradigm says if we work less—spending more time on what we truly love— then we will have less money and financial freedom.

There is an obvious imbalance in this flawed "one way or the other" thinking. Our mission today is to reevaluate what we've been told about money and wealth, opening our eyes to new possibilities and the *vehicle that will bring balance and financial freedom to our lives*. To do this we must rid ourselves of preconceived beliefs regarding money and the accumulation of wealth. The fact is, hardly anybody truly understands money. As a society we live in ignorance. Money is certainly not taught in school. Sure, we're given instructions on how to add, subtract, and divide our money, the beauty of compound interest and supply side economics, but we're not really schooled on the fine art of accumulation. At the end of the day, the sad truth is this: the financial vehicles we are using to drive through life with are broken, and if not broken, they are grossly inadequate to take us where we want to go. Fortunately, all of this is about to change.

The Three Myths of Money

Money Myth #1
Working Hard = Higher Income

If this were true, we'd all be rich. While we can proudly say we are a country with no shortage of hard working people, when we truly start to understand money, we'll see that working hard happens to be the least effective way to make meaningful growth in our income, and perhaps the quickest way to deteriorating health.

Money Myth #2
Education = Higher Income

Universities try to fool you into believing that higher education equals higher earnings. While true to a point, real and life changing income has nothing to do with following the masses into one of the many degree programs now offered. Creating income has more to do with outside-the-box-thinking, and again, with our ability to find ways to work smarter, not harder. In fact, look around and you'll find people who are functionally illiterate earning millions of dollars, while other absolutely brilliant individuals end up flat broke.

Money Myth #3
Time = Money

Like Myth #1, it's not how many hours you spend doing something that will determine your success, but how effective you are in the hours you do spend. Time spent in the vehicle is not nearly as important as the vehicle you have decided to drive. Driving the right vehicle can make you five, ten or twenty times more productive than the individual who in the words of Bruce Springsteen, "Drives all Night."

Three Income Making Strategies

Before we choose the exact vehicle we want to use for our financial journey we should look at our options and the three income-earning strategies (vehicles) to choose from:

Money 1 (M^1)
Money 2 (M^2)
Money 3 (M^3)

If you haven't heard of these terms before, don't worry. You are not alone. Like I just mentioned, you can go right through our educational system, come out with a doctorate's degree in Economics and still know nothing about the art of earning money.

Money 1

M^1 is where a good 96% of our population is coming from. Simply put, *M^1 is the income earning strategy where you trade your time for money.* I replace the brake pads on your Toyota; you give me "X" amount of dollars. I draw up your divorce papers or give your son karate lessons and you pay me an agreed upon fee. While it's an honorable and timeless practice, there is an inherent problem in this strategy. It's called saturation. We simply run out of time. There are only so many hours in a day to make our income. And what happens when we run out of time? We don't have enough dollars to provide for our children's education, to buy the home we always dreamed of, or to retire the way we planned. And if a person does accumulate wealth in this strategy, it is often at the expense of life—our health and happiness.

Money 2

To quote the old cliché, "it takes money to make money." *M^2 is the income earning strategy where you invest money to earn money.* Get yourself a good chunk of change and you can play the stock market, dabble in real estate, commodities and collectibles. And while M^2 is used by only 4% of the population, it is an excellent strategy for creating your financial freedom. Unfortunately, there are a few drawbacks with this vehicle—starting with the fact you have to have the money in the first place. Funny how that works. What's more, you need to be good at using the money you do have or you can be certain it will quickly go away. Also, many of the economic factors that would determine your success in an M^2 vehicle are completely out of your hands. So, while

M^2 is better than M^1, it is still not a guarantee for long term financial success.

Money 3

M^3 is without a doubt the most effective and powerful income earning strategy there is today. It is a strategy of accumulation that wealthy people have been using since ancient Babylonian times. *M^3 is the earning strategy where you multiply your time through the efforts of others by setting up multiple sources of income.* Only 1% of the population uses this strategy and yet they earn 96% of the money. Put another way, M^3 is the art of leveraging the effort of others.

Clearly this is a whole new way of thinking about money. The traditional "old economy" method of making money revolves around the idea of "market share," the concept that to everything there is a limited supply. To illustrate the point the old economy draws up their economic "pie charts." They cut the pie into slices, saying this is my piece of the pie and there is yours. In this old economy scenario, money is finite and if you want more, it means someone else has to get less. Now, I can't speak for everybody, but as far as I'm concerned there are two immediate problems with this scenario. First, I don't believe in finite, and secondly, I don't believe in the idea that "someone else has to have less" in order for "me to get more." It defies the laws of abundance and the power and generosity of the universe to always provide more.

In the new economy, or at least the one intrinsic to an M^3 strategy, we don't deal with limited supply. We deal with infinite supply. If I want more pie for myself, I simply create a larger pie—not taking from my neighbors, but showing them how to expand their own pie. It is a win-win, self-empowering vehicle in which your financial independence is entirely in your own hands. It's not home equity or stock equity. It's people equity. In two short words—it's called Network Marketing—the ultimate M^3 vehicle to get you from A to Z, quickly turning your dreams and visions into reality.

Step 2: Learn to Drive

Once you are fully committed to M^3 and the opportunities it can provide, and once you firmly believe that Network Marketing is the ideal vehicle to launch you into this lucrative world, your next step is simple. You learn to drive.

Surprisingly enough, that's the last thing most people want to do. They don't want to learn to drive; they just want to drive. They don't want to learn how to make money; they just want to make money. But the fact is, you can't run unless you learn to walk and you can't speed ahead to the finish line unless you first learn how to drive. Without knowing the basics, it is impossible to take your game to the next level. In short, learning to drive is tantamount to an athlete working on fundamentals or a musician working on scales—it provides the lifelong tools and foundation to succeed.

Let me make this perfectly clear—this truth applies to you, me and everyone on the Network Marketing team... from top to bottom. There are no exceptions. We all need to learn to drive. What's more, I'm not talking about just getting behind the wheel and putting the foot to the accelerator, but a deeper and more profound mastery of the vehicle we have chosen. In the Network Marketing business, this mastery means we must do two things:

1. We Must Read the Drivers Manual. While virtually everybody has some idea of what Network Marketing is all about, most individuals don't fully understand all the implications and subtleties of its power, and in some cases, limitations. Why? Well, for many of us it's because we got behind the wheel before we learned how to drive—before we read the driver's manual cover-to-cover. We said to ourselves, "I can do this," and jumped right into the Ferrari, not realizing that to get the most out of a Ferrari you need to understand the car from bumper-to-bumper. It is imperative that everyone on your team, starting with yourself, fully understands what Network Marketing is all about. What are the expectations? How will you spend your days? How will you make money? How much money can you make? How long will it take to earn that amount? We need the answer to these and every other question there is to know about the Network Marketing world, then we need to turn around and make sure those that follow us do the same.

I have found that people in this business usually fail not because they lack the proper work habits or skills, but because they lack knowledge and clear expectations. As we begin any new endeavor, there must be no surprises. When we know what is clearly expected of us—what our role is in the overall mission and how we aim to achieve our goals—we will each be able to engage in our journey with the full confidence that our success is inevitable.

2. We Must Get an Instructor. Think back to when you were fifteen years old and you got your learner's permit. Remember how they made you drive in the car with a skilled driver, someone who steered you away from the pitfalls of the road and taught you the ropes? Well, the same principle applies to Network Marketing. Mentorship, sponsorship, teaching—whatever you want to call it—is at the heart and soul of our success. We all need to build on the wisdom of those who have not only read the manual, but live it everyday. Depending on where you are in your networking experience, you will either be given that person or be that person. In either case, it is critical that we understand how important that person is to the success of your team. This instructor will not only offer know-how and expertise on day-to-day activities, but will help manage expectations for your team. He or she will be someone to separate the hype from the reality. Someone to say, "You won't make $3 million in the first three months, but we can offer you this…" The reality an instructor brings to the equation keeps the whole team disciplined and focused. As mentioned before, clear expectations and knowledge is the first line of defense in preventing disinterest and unnecessary burnout. Conversely, a good teacher will help those individuals who are genuinely not interested in Network Marketing move on to something else more quickly. But most importantly, the right instructor will inspire those around him or her to push harder and reach higher than they ever thought they could. This will always be the greatest gift teachers can give their students.

Put it all together and we can see that learning to drive is essential not only for new members, but for all of us. The truth is, of all the great Network Marketers I have seen in my life, there is one consistent trait each and every one of them has in common. To a man and a woman, they have all built their entire organizations on the simple principle that with the right coach or teacher their team can accomplish anything.

Step Three: Put the Right Gas Into the Vehicle

All right, you have chosen the perfect vehicle to make your financial journey. It is M³, and more specifically, Network Marketing. You clearly understand how it works… backwards and forwards…confident that this is the vehicle that is going to help you earn the kind of income that will change your life. Now, it's time to go to the gas station and *fill up the car with gas*. But, before you do remember that the most important element in the equation is not the gas, it's the vehicle.

M³ and Network Marketing is one of the fastest, luxurious and most efficient set of wheels in the world today. It is the Ferrari. The fact is, you could put virtually any type of gas in the vehicle and—if you clearly understand the vehicle as we suggested in step two—it's going to get you to where you want to go faster than 99% of the other vehicles out there. *Yes, the vehicle is that powerful.*

That said, *to get the most out of your vehicle*, you still have to pick the right gas. The right, high-octane gas will not only get your vehicle moving, but also will double and even triple your effectiveness and rate of success. It will make your vehicle faster, more efficient, and last longer.

So, what kind of gas do you put in your vehicle? Well, there are a lot of Network Marketing opportunities out there— from Amway to Xango. While they all have their advantages and disadvantages, for my money USANA is the best gas on the market today. Like any good gas, I don't need to think about it. I not only believe in the quality of their products, but in the integrity of the organization and the people who serve it. What's more, I am proud to be a contributing factor in helping those around me in their quest to achieve optimal health. While I'm obviously prejudiced I believe that with a close inspection, you too will be convinced that USANA is the only gas for the Ferrari called Network Marketing. Of course, at the end of the day, whatever gas you choose to put into your vehicle, make sure it's the best you can get your hands on. Make sure you believe in the people as well as the organization, and that you can stand confidently behind everything it represents and professes to be.

Step Four: Go Back to School

You've read the manual and think you've learned all there is to know about Network Marketing…and now here I am saying you have to go back to school. Yes, I am. But remember, I'm also promising the potential to reach financial freedom faster than 99% of the rest of the world and—like all meaningful achievement—that comes with a price. First off, let's talk about going back to school and what that means. For those of us in Network Marketing:

- *Going Back to School* is our commitment to the simple idea that we should always be reaching for the next level.

- *Going Back to School* is our commitment to life long education and growth.

- *Going Back to School* is an understanding that our

evolvement and rate of success, like all schooling, will always be in direct proportion to our individual effort (how many classes we take, how hard we study, prepare and are willing to go the extra mile).

• *Going Back to School*, most importantly, is the *approach we take* to reach our success. It is not only a method of study, but the *mindset of how we will learn and grow our business.*

Sponsor, Teaching and the Role of Education in Network Marketing

Sponsor and teach. They are two of the most important words in Network Marketing. In fact, this is not so much a sponsor business as it is a sponsor and teaching business, which is why teachers typically do so well in our field. And just what are we trying to teach, and for that matter, where are we trying to take our team in the first place?

Our initial aim in Network Marketing is three fold: We want to 1. Expose. 2. Involve and 3. Upgrade. The first objective is to get someone exposed to our business. Once they are comfortable in the world, then we can get them involved and as their enthusiasm increases and their income grows, we need to upgrade them from a few hundred dollars a month to a few thousand dollars a month. Now, the question arises: What does it take to get a person properly involved in the business? I'll tell you and you can pin this onto your bulletin board and take it straight to the bank: **It takes education, time and a "Go Back to School" mentality**.

It is important to understand that it will take most people between three to six months to begin earning significant money. Unfortunately, most people bring their contacts into the business with the faulty misconception that they are going to make a lot of money right away. That is simply irresponsible and does a disservice to us all.

For someone to succeed they need to build a strong foundation. After all, you can't build a skyscraper until you start laying the concrete and steel that will support your building for years to come. The same is true in Network Marketing. You must lay a strong foundation before you will see the financial fruits of your labor. This takes time. Our individual mission is to make ourselves and our teams feel comfortable with this start up time, which is why I refer to this phase as a period of Going Back to School. It should be exciting and exploratory, with the promise of riches upon graduation.

Of course, there will always be those individuals who will balk at the idea of school and education. They want riches and they want them now. And while we can certainly admire their ambition and pluck, we must make them (and ourselves) understand the value of a strong foundation—"that dues need to be paid." And to all these individuals, there is only one simple question to ask. "Do you know of any school, college, or educational system in the world where you can graduate in four years, then hope to retire in one to three years at better than $150,000 a year?" Ask them that and you usually get dead silence. It all starts to make sense. Especially when you consider that most people go to college so they can get a better job, work 30 to 40 years and then retire on half of what they couldn't afford to live on for the first 30 to 40 years.

There is no doubt about it, the payoff of Network Marketing is enormous. But it requires that we learn. It requires this Back to School mentality. And to drive this point home, we can learn a little from our M^1 and M^2 friends. If you were to ask a professional lawyer or doctor when they started practicing their profession, they'd tell you the day they got out of school. Now, ask a Network Marketer when they started practicing their profession and they'll tell you from the moment they signed their application. Now, you can start to see what is wrong with our industry. People actually think they can get into this business and make money before they learn what to do. It is like the student studying to be a brain surgeon; suddenly deciding he's going to do a few operations before he graduates. Make a little beer money. I don't think so. And while in Network Marketing we can certainly start to make money right away to build a true and life changing income, it takes time, learning and education.

Think about it. For those of you who went to school, how much money did you make while you spent four years earning your degree? You didn't make anything, right? You just spent money, studied, took tests and learned. So, why should a person in Network Marketing be concerned about making money in the first three to six months when they have the potential to retire in one to three years? We need to get this message across to everyone. Your success depends on it.

We also need to get across what this "schooling" looks like and the commitment it will require. Of course, the schooling I'm talking about is the school of enrollment. You're going through our system, reading our books, listening to audio presentations and watching training videos. You're meeting with your coach or colleagues, joining in teleconferences and training sessions. Practicing your pitches. Mastering everything there is to know about your specific Network Marketing business.

And how long will it take? Well, it's different for everybody. The same way one person will graduate from a traditional college in four years, someone else will take three years or seven years. It all depends on the time and commitment you put in to it. If you only take three classes a week, it's going to take longer. Same thing with Network Marketing. How soon do you want to start earning money? It all depends on when you want your degree…two years? Four years? eight years? Again, it's up to you.

Ultimately, I believe if an individual was willing to go back to school for ten to fifteen hours a week for three to six months, they could learn everything they need to build a lucrative Network Marketing enterprise, retiring on a six-figure income in one to three years. Of course, there are no guarantees. You still have to do the work. You still have to follow through with action. And that also takes time.

In fact, if you're in this business to achieve lasting financial independence, you will have to make a two to three year commitment to follow through with everything you learned. Now, what if you don't want to make that type of commitment? What are your options? Well, you could go back to working 30 to 40 years for someone else's dream. In other words, there are no options.

Go to school for three to six months, then make a two to five year commitment and you will inevitably see the level of success and benefits this business can bring. You will no longer be paying for your success, you'll be enjoying the benefits of your success…and all the friendships, freedom, money, personal growth, and security that comes with it.

Step Four: Find New Drivers

The number one question I get asked every day is this: "How do I approach my friends and contacts about this business? How do I get new students? How do I find new drivers? Should I talk about the company, the products or the marketing plan?" They are all good questions and our success hinges on our answers. Bottom line, in order for Network Marketing to survive, we need new drivers. Unfortunately, after going to the dentist and public speaking, selling is probably our next greatest fear. Unless you are a born and bred Wily Loman type, most of us cringe at the thought of having to sell anything—whether it's our self, a product or an opportunity.

And this might be true for those of us in Network Marketing as well, if it weren't for the fact that we're not just selling products, we're selling opportunities...opportunities for people to improve their lives—to experience the wealth and financial freedom they've never experienced before. And when you do that everything sells itself. It's a matter of laying down the facts and letting whomever you're talking to make the choice. It is selling without the twisting arms we traditionally equate to sales. In short, it's a matter of approach. And just what is that approach?

You start where we all start—by putting down a list of four serious business partners you want to build a home based business with. Find those people, then ask this simple question. "If you could be earning between $2,000 and $6,000 per month on top of what you are currently earning, could you see yourself going back to school for three to six months to learn how to do it?" You tell them they don't need to be a salesperson, they don't need a lot of education and they certainly don't need a lot of money. Oh, and by the way, if they follow your system, they could easily retire in three years with a powerful residual stream of income. Put it that way and watch how people lean forward, their eyes lighting up. And once they're interested, you show them the curriculum or prospecting pack, then guide them to their classroom and the teacher or sponsor that will show them the rest of the way. It's that easy. And if they're not interested, you move on to the next prospect.

The   key is to keep it simple—presenting a clear opportunity for your prospects to get back the life that, in most of their cases, has slipped away. You see, most people, after sleep, commuting, work time and all the other commitments they have each day, barely have two hours a day they can truly call their own. They are slaves to their jobs and their M[1] lifestyle. What you're doing is helping them find a solution to their lack of control, bringing not only money and financial freedom into their lives, but balance and health. And that is the easiest sale in the world.

Now, once you have your four new drivers, the next critical step—one that is missed by so many in this business—is to create a mindset that you are now in a *partnership with these four individuals*. Each one of these individuals must know that you are fully committed to spending 25% of your next two years to helping them succeed.

What happens next? Those four individuals will lead you to another four individuals underneath them and another four underneath them and another four underneath them.

And when you have sixteen fully committed individuals, guess what? Do you get the picture? Remember, if you can lock in emotionally with these four people over the next two years, you will find that you can achieve all the dreams you ever wanted.

Finally, let me say one more thing about the whole sales thing. There is a philosophy I live and breathe by, one that I wholeheartedly attribute to my success. It is this: I have never in my Network Marketing career found myself looking at this business and the need for getting new drivers as a matter of sales...a drive to get people to sign on the dotted line. Rather, I have always looked at my mission in Network Marketing as a journey to help others achieve their goals. This isn't just about me getting to the top; it's about taking my friends, family and associates with me. It's about helping others enjoy the same M^3 lifestyle I enjoy.

I have watched those around me struggle with their M^1 lifestyle, being slaves to their jobs and financial conditions, unable to find the joy and purpose they deserve. And I have found great personal satisfaction in helping these individuals find a way out of the darkness and limitations of M^1 and into the light and promise of M^3.

I don't call that sales. I call it changing lives. That is the power of Network Marketing and the power of the **Driver's Formula for Success.**

*If you go to work
on your goals,
your goals will
go to work on
you. If you go
to work on your
plan, your plan
will go to work
on you. Whatever
good things we
build end up
building us.*

— Jim Rohn

Chapter Six
Doing The Right Things Consistently
The 3 Steps to Success

Over the years I've helped many people reach their goals and while the lives of these people were certainly enriched by the experience, I believe my life was equally enriched. Not just through the gift of being able to help others achieve their dreams, but through the experiences and lessons I've learned along the way.

Over time, I have developed these lessons into powerful principles that have helped me grow my business and countless other people grow theirs. In fact, I've narrowed down my success in Network Marketing to three fundamental steps. I call them appropriately enough, *"The 3 Steps to Success."* Nothing fancy, just simple, everyday common sense. I'm going to share these steps with you in this chapter, but before I do I want you to understand the underlying principles behind this business. I want you to see for yourself just how truly remarkable it is that an entire industry's success can be reduced to three simple steps.

Today, the Network Marketing industry is a true profession. It's not a hobby, an also-ran or some half-baked, get rich scheme. It's a multi-billion dollar business with some of the most gifted business minds in the world now a part of it. That wasn't always so. In fact, this industry just a few years ago was still pretty much in its infancy. It's been called Multi-Level Marketing, Distribution Networking and Direct Selling. Whatever the name, Network Marketing has now arrived as a full-fledged, viable path to success. Its doors are open to virtually anyone who chooses to walk through them.

Paul Zane Pilzer, a New York Times bestselling author, recently wrote a book called *The Next Millionaire.* In his book, Pilzer states that "direct selling is the perfect intellectual distribution business for today's economy. The modern direct selling industry is poised to become the distribution method of choice for all new products and services, and for most people, the only way they're ever going to accumulate a significant amount of wealth through passive income." As Pilzer points out, the wealth opportunity of Network Marketing is immense, but what's truly amazing about this industry is that it's open to anyone and everyone. While you may need years of education to work in a corporation, to work for yourself in Network Marketing you only need the desire to succeed. Nothing more. No degree. No second mortgage. No rich uncle. Just you and the *3 Steps to Success*—three basic principles that are time tested and proven to work. Best of all, they are easy to implement and duplicate, which is the ultimate key to success in this industry.

Whatever it is that you and I do to build our organization, everyone in the organization has to be able to do it as well. Whether they have our intelligence or not, whether they have our education or not, whether they have our personality, particular skills and abilities or not, even whether they live in our part of the country or not—everyone has to be able to build the business the same exact way. Our business has to be, to coin a word, "duplicatable." After all, if you or I do something to succeed that no one else can do, then we won't be able to expand our business. We'll be tied to our business by virtue of the fact that no one else can make it work. But, if we can make our business easy to duplicate, we can recruit an unlimited number of people to generate income for us and for themselves. It cannot be said often enough or loud enough, but this is the single most valuable element of Network Marketing.

That's what my *3 Steps To Success* will do. They will make your business strategy easy to implement and easy to duplicate. You don't have to concoct a grand scheme, you don't have to outwit your competitors, you don't have to develop a proprietary strategy and you certainly don't have to get bogged down in trying to build a better mousetrap. You just have to follow the steps—one by one—with the confidence that you are laying the foundation that will build your business and shape your dreams.

Prerequisite To The 3 Simple Steps

If you chase two rabbits, both will escape.
— Anonymous

Just like in college, before you can learn one thing, you have to first learn another. Each lesson we take should set the foundation to make sure the next lesson is properly received and understood. And so before I introduce the *3 Steps To Success*, I want you to do one thing. I want you to read *Think And Grow Rich* by Napoleon Hill. It's an absolute must. If you've already read it, read it again. Some of the greatest minds of our time have read this book and they've all said pretty much the same thing. It can change your life. In fact, you should read all the motivational and inspirational books you can get your hands on. They'll raise your consciousness, uplift, inspire, and help you attract success into your life.

But most importantly, make sure you start with *Think And Grow Rich*. In his book, Napoleon Hill outlines his principles of success. He calls them dynamic principles. For our purposes and the work we'll be doing with the *3 Steps To Success*, there is one principle Hill speaks about that is more important than any other—it's called "singleness of purpose."

Hopefully by now, you're ready to make the commitment to redefine your dreams and do everything possible to make those dreams reality. No matter what it is in life you want, the *3 Steps To Success* will enable you to successfully write your own future—to receive the things in life you want the most. But to do this, you have to have singleness of purpose.

Let me share with you what singleness of purpose means. Whatever company you align yourself with in this industry you have to believe in its power and potential. You have to believe it's the best opportunity you have to achieve financial independence—anywhere and anyplace in the world. If you do not intensely believe this, you will never be able to receive the joy and benefits a business of this magnitude can deliver. If you can't say with 100% conviction that this is an opportunity that will change your life you're doomed from the start.

Of course, if you can't say that about your current organization it's not too late to find another. There are many great opportunities in Network Marketing…you just have to be willing to do your homework to find one. It's called research and due diligence. I certainly did my research. I put in long, tedious hours to find exactly what I was looking for and, at the end of the day, I clearly found the company that has enabled me to realize my dreams. Remember, you can never be more successful than the company you associate yourself with. In my case, it was Dr. Myron Wentz and the USANA global vision that I knew I had to follow.

The reason you have to believe in your company is simple math. If you're going to be spending countless hours, days, weeks, months and years on growing your home based business, it better be with a company that will yield results to match the effort.

I often see people go to home based business expos and spend thousands of dollars on various courses and programs they believe will get them rich. Often times, it doesn't even matter if they believe in the businesses or not. It's a lottery mentality, and I'll tell you this, it's a disaster waiting to happen. You can't succeed in this business with a smorgasbord approach, playing every opportunity that comes your way in the hopes that one will hit. If there's anything in this book that I want you to clearly understand it is this: *you'll never achieve your financial dreams until you pick one thing and stick with it.*

Truth is, I have people wanting to share their home based business opportunities with me all the time. While, I respect each one of them for their courage to share what they believe is the right program for them, I constantly remind myself of Napoleon Hill's powerful message. You see, it's not that these other programs are bad, it's that my success has been founded on "singleness of purpose." If I were hopping around from business to business or trying to manage two or more business opportunities at a time, I'd certainly fail. Instead, I determined that nothing, absolutely nothing would distract me from my chief aim in life. My effort, my heart, my time, my emotions and my money are all in one place...building my USANA business!

Unfortunately, most people are more than ready and willing to bounce from one opportunity to the next. It's the get rich quick mentality. They want to succeed fast, and they become discouraged and discontent when their results don't immediately match their misguided expectations.

It reminds me of the Chinese Bamboo Tree. You plant a seed and in the first year, you water and fertilize it...water and fertilize, water, and fertilize. And nothing happens. Then during the second year you water and fertilize it again...water and fertilize, water and fertilize. Still nothing happens. During the third year you do the same water and fertilize routine, and again nothing happens. The same thing continues during the fourth, fifth and sixth years. But in the seventh year a miracle happens. Within a twenty-one day period, the Chinese Bamboo Tree grows to over 80 feet. Imagine 80 feet in just three weeks. It is an incredible feat of beauty and power.

Of course, the question needs to be asked. "Did the Chinese Bamboo Tree grow 80 feet in twenty-one days or in seven years?" It looked like it grew in twenty-one days, but ask any horticulturist and they'll tell you that the bamboo tree would have died if, in any one year you didn't water and fertilize it *over and over again*. And of course, your business is the same way. It also needs to be watered and fertilized... not once, but again and again. It needs to be tended and cared for—and all without you demanding that it give back to you immediately.

It's called "Doing the right thing long enough consistently" and it's the magical, life-changing phrase that makes this whole entire Network Marketing industry work. It's a simple, repeatable system of water and fertilize and like the great Chinese Bamboo Tree, it will not disappoint. Keep at it and I guarantee you will enjoy your own "twenty-one days of growth." All it takes is a singleness of purpose.

The 3 Steps To Success

> *A straight path never leads anywhere except to the objective.*
> — André Gide

Here's the beauty of the *3 Steps To Success*. Most of what you need to know we've already learned in this book. Now we simply have to put it into a concrete and repeatable system. While many people try to complicate this the steps are actually very basic and straightforward.

The 3 Steps To Success

1. Find A Prospect To Show Your Business To
2. Show Your Opportunity To That Person
3. When They Join, Help Them

Does it seem too simple? Too easy? Well, I'll tell you this and it comes from my experiences—execute these steps over and over again, and you will succeed in this business like never before. Teach your team to execute on these steps and the reaches of your wealth and success will be endless.

Are there other elements involved? Of course. As we've

discussed already, you need to—

- Have A Dream
- Discover Your Why
- Declare Your Vision
- Define Your Leadership Role
- Build Relationships With One Another

While we've already discussed the first four elements at length, the fifth, *Building Relationships With One Another*, is new. It involves the friendships and relationships you develop in the course of building your business. There is no amount of financial compensation that equals the personal satisfaction one gains from extending a hand, opening the heart and making a life changing contribution to another individual. In fact, this mindset is vitally important to the essence and longevity of this business. We are in a people centric business and the strength of the personal relationships we have will directly affect the financial compensation we earn. It's what makes our business so unique and is the core reason for its universal and global acceptance.

Of course, it's not just the financial gain that's rewarding, it's also the personal joy and fulfillment these relationships bring. My top leaders and I are more than business associates. We are friends and confidantes. We share both work and play, our struggles and our joys. Even our vacations. If I ever need anything, no matter how big or small, I know I can pick up the phone and call any one of them, and they'll drop what they're doing to help me out just as I would for them. Yes, the financial rewards in this business are terrific. But nothing, absolutely nothing comes close to the personal relationships that you will enjoy each day you're in this business.

With these five elements in mind, let's take a closer look

at the *3 Steps To Success.*

Step #1 - Find A Prospect To Show Your Business To

It is said that the life force of any organization is the new blood that you bring to it. In other words, your success will be directly tied to your ability to share your unique business opportunity with new blood, also called the *prospect.* There are only four primary ways to get prospects. Although, many people will spend time and energy trying to come up with new ideas for prospecting, spinning their wheels as they look for something that's not there. In truth, it's really a simple and straightforward process. None of these four ideas are terribly new but all of them work. So, rather than try to reinvent the wheel just execute this step using any or all of the four suggested ways:

1. The first way to get prospects is to focus on your warm market. Yes, your friends, neighbors and relatives. Now, I can hear your thoughts already. "I already talked to my warm market and they are not interested." Well, maybe they're not or maybe you're simply scared and uneasy with the idea of talking to your close acquaintances about this business. Either way, you need to get past these self-defeating thoughts. This is a critical element in your business building process and one that is quite simple, once you have the proper coaching, mentoring and leadership support.

2. The second way to get prospects is to find them while you are out living life. These are the people you run across everyday—at the bank, the cleaners, the coffee house, PTA meetings and little league. I understand this can be hard. I also understand that prospecting by its very nature is difficult for most people, and prospecting strangers can be entirely frightful. My recommendation here is to not look at these people as strangers. Look at them as future friends. Trust me, that's what they're going to become...once you offer them the opportunity to change their lives and to create the wealth and freedom that only personal success can bring. Suddenly the strangers on the street will become your friends and partners in success.

3. The third type of prospecting is to control the way a prospect sees the business. Now I realize this is more of a method of prospecting than it is an actual way to prospect, but I believe it is important enough to warrant its own heading. In fact, we must understand this principle to move forward. Suppose you're a businessperson and you see a card in a telephone booth that says, "Get rich...Call me for the opportunity of a lifetime." You might be curious and you might even call. The only problem is, you're going to think that in order to be successful in this business you'll have to put business cards in telephone booths all over the place, and field calls from strangers at all hours of the night. You see, the people on your team will do exactly what they see you do. However you expose people to your business is exactly what they think they will have to do to be successful. And here's the problem— 99% of the time it's not duplicatable. So rather than prospect in ways that can't be duplicated or in ways that might turn people off, you need to communicate your opportunity in a way that is duplicatable. It's that simple. While there are many duplicatable methods to communicate your opportunity—live events, brochures and phone calls—one of the best is the live webcast presentation. It's an idea that was taught to me that's turnkey and can easily be duplicated by anyone.

*4. The fourth method of prospecting is to use the Internet and online methodologies. In other words, use **live webcasts**.* Dr. Denis Waitley has said, "If you're not online, you'll be in the bread line." No truer words have been spoken.

Step # 2 - Show Your Opportunity To That Person

Once you have a prospect, the next step is to show that person your opportunity. Showing your opportunity has to be standardized. It has to be virtually the same every time for every person. That means the same presentation no matter who's watching it, and the same presentation no matter who's giving it. Why? Because the presentation is carefully outlined to cover all of the right hot buttons in the exact order that delivers the desired results. The presentation has been developed based on actual success and failure experiences, and it's engineered to deliver a predictable and successful outcome consistently. In other words, it takes all of the guesswork out of the equation. It's proven to work. You can't beat that.

Suprisingly, some people do try to beat it. In fact, I've coached people who say they've shown their own version of the opportunity over 20 times yet have not successfully sponsored anyone. I then find out that every time they show their presentation, it's different. They try to wing it so their presentations unravel as they jump from topic to topic. It's confusing, unattractive and choppy. Not only is this a recipe for failure, but even if this style of presentation did work once in a while, it's not duplicatable.

We need to establish a strong, well-developed presentation and deliver it the same way every time, maximizing our desired objective and ensuring that all prospects enjoy and understand the power of what we do.

Step #3 - When They Join, Help Them

At various steps throughout this book, we've discussed the importance of developing your team. If there's any business you can't do it alone in, it's this one. By developing your team, you not only increase their chances of success, but you also increase your own.

It can be an exhilarating experience to enroll a new prospect into your business. They're excited, and you've taken one of the most critical steps towards your success—building your team. But, your work doesn't stop there. You may be so inspired by your prospecting success that you want to run out and start prospecting some more. After all, you found the key to success, and now you figure all you have to do is sign up more people and you're on your way.

While it's true, you do need to continually build your team, you also need to nurture and develop the team members you already have. Like customers, it's much easier to help a current team member succeed than it is to find a new one, so treat your team members like a valuable investment and do what it takes to make them succeed. That may be training, it may be handholding or it may be teaching them to proficiently execute the *3 Steps To Success*. It's a simple step that will reap enormous and lifelong rewards.

Help people succeed, and they'll help you succeed in return.

As I write this book, the Network Marketing industry is heading full speed ahead towards the biggest boom of all time. If you follow the *3 Steps To Success*, you will be at the forefront of this growth. If you can apply this singleness of purpose to your business and do the right thing consistently, you will succeed in this industry, with the least degree of effort and the greatest degree of results.

*All men should
strive to learn
before they die,
what they are
running from, and
to, and why.*

— James Thurber

Chapter Seven
Discovering What Matters Most
The Art of the First Contact

In the last chapter we talked about finding prospects and the need to effectively present our opportunities to those prospects. In this chapter we'll talk about what that means. How do we approach our prospects? How do we make contact? How do we get our prospects out of their busy lives long enough to preview our program, to hear what we have to say, to see that we are presenting an opportunity that could change their lives?

Make no mistake about it—the challenge is great. People are busy, scared, stuck, and stubborn. People don't have time to work on their life. In other words, they can't be bothered sharpening their axe because they're so busy chopping wood.

What I'm going to share with you now is a step-by-step formula on how to successfully make "first contact" with your potential home based business prospects. For most of us this is a daunting task. We've never been properly taught on how to successfully introduce our prospects to their home based business enterprise. Well, all that's about to change.

But before we begin, I think it is important to mention a few simple realities that might help make your first contact successful.

Reality Number One—People Are Busy.

We need to recognize that in the beginning of this contact phase your prospects may very well view your presentation as nothing more than one giant distraction. We must be respectful of their time, careful to accommodate their schedules and demands. More importantly, we must be ready with our presentations, making sure they are thorough, polished and precise.

Reality Number Two—People Do Have Valid Objections.

Maybe the objections aren't valid for you or me, but for where your prospect is at that particular moment in his or her life, it is perfectly understandable. The last thing we want to do is deny someone else their own experience—to tell them how to feel. In fact, we want your prospects to have those objections. And here is the key—the objections your prospects have will often show them the opportunities more clearly.

Reality Number Three—People Will Say No.

The experienced business builder will recognize that

this is a process of sorting through different people and their individual needs. Rejection should never be taken personally. Yes, your prospect may say, "No" and actually mean it, but just as often, they may say "No," when they really mean, "Not right now," or "I don't understand what you're talking about." We have to remember that "no" is often an important step in the road to "yes." In fact, I know of many talented and highly successful network marketers who began their careers with that same "no."

So, back to the original question. How do you approach and make contact with your prospect? Simple. You put together a compelling presentation that not only answers your prospect's basic questions, but supplies them with enough information and facts that it would make it inconceivable for them to not want to get involved and join the program. In other words, it's the presentation, presentation and presentation.
I've worked with many teams over the years and almost all of them struggle in one specific area—they don't deliver a compelling or powerful presentation. And because of that, they don't achieve the level of success that they desire. Well, we can't afford to let that happen, so I've put together a step-by-step formula to create a presentation that you can immediately put to use.

Here is the caveat—in order for it to work, it must be used properly. The best presentation is useless if you don't take the time to master it. Lance Armstrong could have had all the technical skills and know-how in the world, but if he didn't go out and ride his bike every day—if he didn't practice his art—he would have never succeeded to the degree he did. He would have never won seven Tour de Frances. Your presentation will only be successful if you practice it to the point of perfection. I call it "effortless mastery." While, that might sound like an oxymoron, actors, politicians and presenters have been using it for ages. Effortless means something "automatic with ease," while mastery means something "that goes beyond practicing." In other words, you need to practice your presentations so much that it seems— not that you have memorized it—but that you are saying it for the first time and doing it with effortless mastery. That is how you bring energy and vitality to your presentation.

I've had the good fortune to learn the skills necessary to becoming great at sponsoring. I've been recognized many times for my success. But I'm not successful at it by accident. I have put a lot of time into it. I know exactly what I'm going to say. I can shift gears…you can ask me questions...stop me...and I'll pick it right back up where I left off. All because I have programmed myself to do it. I have trained myself.

And that is exactly where you need to get with your own presentations—not having to think about them. Call it effortless mastery or any other name. In either case, you must work on the presentation I am about to offer until it is a part of every fiber of your being. So polish your mirror and let's begin.

The Art of the First Contact

The greatest compliment that was ever paid me was when someone asked me what I thought, and attended to my answer.
— Henry David Thoreau

In the world of Network Marketing all effective presentations should have one thing in common. They should work for anyone. They should be equally appropriate for a corporate executive or a waiter, a PhD or a soccer mom. It doesn't matter. Certainly we will need to tailor our presentation to different individual needs, but the principle and process should remain the same. Regardless of the individual we are talking to we are taking them all on the same journey.

This journey can be broken into seven stages we must take our prospect through. I have presented these stages as questions, for invariably, they are what your prospects will want to know to move forward, whether they verbalize the question or not. Remember we must go through all the stages to be successful. You don't want to just jump in and start bombarding them with your opportunity and some never-before-seen product that they don't have any reason to care about yet. Take it slowly, step-by-step.

So with that in mind, we begin with the first, and arguably, most important stage.

Stage One
What do I want out of life?

The first stage in your contact presentation is to always find out what matters most to your prospect. Until we identify with their needs and what is important to them they are not going to be interested in going any further with the process. It's like that old saying, "People don't care what we know until they know we care." Put another way, it doesn't matter what *we* care about, only what *they* care about. This is very important for us to understand, because at this point, your prospects are not remotely interested in your company. They don't care that your opportunity is transforming lives. They don't care that your company is debt free. They don't care that they can earn a lot of money using your company's marketing plan. They don't care about any of those things until you start to focus on what they want—then and only then—will they be able to see the opportunity of Network Marketing.

So how do we get them to this point? How do we find out what's important to them? We do it through the *Discovery Process*. The *Discovery Process* is just what its name implies. It is a process where, **through specific and targeted questions**, we take our prospects through a personal journey from where they are today to where they would like to be tomorrow. By asking them precise questions you will find clues about the different areas you may be able to help them with.

One of the first things in the process that I try to find out is whether the person I'm talking to is really doing what they want to be doing with their life. For instance, I might say, "Ginny, I understand you're really busy and I appreciate that. In fact, that's the reason I called. It's about your time. Are you doing the things you really want to do? And are you happy with what you're doing?"

Now don't be surprised if you get an "everything's great" answer. That's perfectly fine because, remember, we're just starting the relationship-building process. However, even if they give you the "everything's fine" response, I would still continue to ask them the questions, only in different ways. Sooner or later, you will break through to something they would like to change. The idea here is to find out what makes them tick. What are some of their hot buttons? In other words, what makes them do what they're doing? More importantly, we need to bring them face to face with the reality of what they are doing and the impact it has made on their life, whether positive or negative.

Your ultimate aim is to lead your prospects to the realization that what they are currently doing in their life is not what they would really like to be doing...and the only reason they don't do anything about it is because they are so caught up in everyday life that they simply can't see the forest for the trees.

We can look for our prospect's hot buttons by giving them some verbal hints that might get them to talk about what it is that's bothering them. Now, most of us approach this from the wealth angle, the prospect's lack of money and financial freedom. While this is certainly most individuals' number one concern, fortunately, in this industry we have a philosophy that encompasses more than the financial issues facing us today. There are many motivators for what we do, so there should, likewise, be a number of ways that we can introduce our program to our prospects.

I call these motivators the *Six Areas of Life Balance*. Once again, they have each been put in the form of a question, reminding us that, in this *Discovery Process*, our goal is to seek answers and the first thing we want to know is: **what matters to them?**

Remember, understanding who you're talking to and what's important to them will allow you to successfully stimulate conversation in several areas.

The Six Areas of Life Balance

1. Do you have the Physical health you want? Do you have the energy and vitality to enjoy the things most important to you? Or does your job tire you out and wear you down?

2. Do you have the peace of mind and emotional health you want? Are you content with what you have? Are you doing the things in life you always dreamed of doing? Are you happy, satisfied and content? Or stressed, anxious and angry?

3. Do you have the relationships you want? Do you spend as much quality time with your family and friends as you'd like to? Are you isolated? Lonely? Too busy to share your life with someone?

4. Do you have the career you want? Do you like how you earn your living? Does your work challenge you? Does it allow you to give, share and help those around you? Do you make a difference in the world?

5. Do you have the inner life you want? Whatever path you choose to express yourself, do you have adequate time for it, time to feed your spirit and nurture your soul?

6. Do you have the financial freedom you want? While I have saved this for last—if I had to pinpoint the most basic issue for 98% of the people I meet—it would be finances. Face it, people are financially struggling everywhere you look, which is why this is the most common and valuable entry point in our contact with prospects. What's more, and I cannot emphasize this strongly enough, our financial freedom affects the other five areas of our life balance.

As you work your way through this *Discovery Process*, understanding who you are talking to and what's important to them will allow you to successfully find your prospects' hot buttons, which is the entry point to truly realizing what matters most to them. And, once you have identified this, you can move on to the next stage...letting the prospect know what matters to you.

Stage Two
Why am I doing this?

This is, without a doubt, one of the most powerful parts of the presentation. Surprisingly, not many people take the time to teach this part of the formula. It's called *your personal story—who you are and why you're doing this*. It is during this stage when the relationship building process really starts to develop when it becomes strong and your prospect starts to believe you "truly care."

If you properly introduce your prospect to your personal story you will instantly create the desire in him or her to hear about your opportunity. I'm telling you, it's a lot easier to talk about your program when the person sitting across from you—or on the other end of the telephone—actually wants to hear the details.

Your personal story has three parts—your childhood, teen and adult years. Now, obviously you're not going to give your prospect your entire "womb-to-this-moment" history, but you will want to share those events that helped shape who you are today. You'll want to share your own struggles with finances, relationships, and career; your own quest to find balance and purpose in your life. While your individual story will be unique to you, your prospect will undoubtedly be able to identify with many of the same struggles and challenges.

What's important to understand, and sometimes hard to accept, is you don't have to know very much about your company's products or marketing in order to become extremely successful at building your Network Marketing business. People do business, at least in the beginning, with people they like, trust and believe in. Not companies, their products or commission schedules. The people you share your opportunity with will be far more impressed by you if you share what your dreams are, than they would be by your ability to recite product ingredients and marketing strategies.

Perhaps the greatest thing about this stage is you don't need to be an expert to start sharing your story. All you need is to be open, honest and genuine.

Stage Three
What kind of industry am I in & how does it work?

If you've been doing your job right, sooner or later, your prospects are going to want to know more. They're going to want to know what kind of industry you're in. What kind of business you're involved in. Of course, your answer is simple. "Network Marketing," which you would probably want to follow up with, "Do you know anything about it?"

At this point, your prospect would say they do or they

don't. If they do, you've got it made and you can either skip the next section or you can recap with an abbreviated explanation. I have found that it can sometimes be helpful to have them share with you their thoughts and feelings as to their understanding of the system. You may find that two powerful things will begin to develop if you do:

> 1. They will share with you their personal feelings as to what they found valuable going through the system, which is extremely beneficial in the *Discovery Process.*

> 2. They will begin to internalize their own words... and those words can become a powerful motivator for them. Soon, they will actually start convincing *you* that *they* are the perfect candidates for your program. If you try this occasionally in your presentation I believe you may find it a compelling and valuable method of connecting with your potential business partners on a more intimate level.

Now, of course, when they say they don't know anything about Networking Marketing, or very little, it's time to enlighten them. Remember, as you explain the way Network Marketing works, you're not only trying to educate and inform, but to get them excited and pumped...and to do it in a way that will remove any and all objections they may have. The six main objectives a prospect may have are:

> 1. Is this a pyramid?
> 2. Is this something I can get passionate about?
> 3. Do I have to recruit my friends, neighbors and relatives?
> 4. Is this something I can afford to do financially?
> 5. Do I have to be a salesperson?

6. Do you provide adequate training?

So how do we get rid of these objections, while simultaneously pumping up our prospect? We do it with the *Strawberry Story* and *The Perfect One Liner*. These two magical concepts, that were originally developed and taught by Tom "Big Al" Schreiter, have made it possible for thousands to learn the skills necessary to building a thriving home-based business. If you use these two concepts I can promise you success.

The Strawberry Story

This story, if told right, will immediately get rid of your number one "Is this a pyramid?" objection. It's a very simple "How a strawberry gets to market" story that also explains the three major benefits of owning your own Network Marketing business. The exchange might go something like this:

> A strawberry is picked in a field and then sold to a local co-op. The local co-op would then sell it to a National Broker who would then sell it to Safeway. Safeway will then distribute it to all its warehouses. The warehouse loads up a truck and delivers the strawberry to the local Safeway store and the local Safeway store would mark up the strawberry by 30%-40% to pay for overhead—employee salaries, utilities, insurance and the like. And, of course, at the end of the day, the consumer gets his strawberry and everybody's happy. That's how the retail market works and how we buy 99% of everything that is in our life today.

Network Marketing works a little bit different. It's just a more direct way of getting product to the ultimate consumer and it works like this. The strawberry is picked in the field and is purchased directly by the Network Marketing Company. The Network Marketing Company will then allow its business partners to purchase the strawberry at wholesale. Now how would you rather buy your products—wholesale or retail? Of course, wholesale.

And that is the primary reason why people join us and decide to start their own home based business. Of course, there is a second reason why people join us...and that reason is to buy products at wholesale and to then share them with others who would like to purchase them from us. That's called retail profit. Make a few hundred extra dollars a month, right? Not that you have to. It's entirely your choice. You do or you don't.

And with that, the light bulb in your prospects head usually switches on. They realize that while they may not choose to sell their product, if the opportunity arises, they could do it. It's a pressure free, anxiety free proposition. Add it all up and in one quick story, you have demystified and explained the world of Network Marketing...removing all thoughts of pyramids.

The Perfect One Liner

Of course, there is one other way to demystify and explain the world of Network Marketing. In fact, it not only explains

Network Marketing, it eliminates the prospect's objections and builds immediate confidence. I call it the *Perfect One Liner.* I believe that if you use this powerful first sentence to open your presentations with, you could literally screw up the rest of the presentation and still sponsor your potential prospect. You could talk about the wrong products, say our companies name backwards, turn the compensation plan upside down and still get your potential prospect to join. However, if you don't have this powerful sentence, you could walk on water and your prospect wouldn't be interested.

This first sentence needs to be powerful. It should not only eliminate all objections, but it should get the prospect pumped, excited and wanting to join. Most of all, this first sentence should make the prospect feel confident that this is something he or she can easily accomplish.

What is that first sentence?

"Most people do Network Marketing everyday, but they just don't get paid for it."

It is a simple, sweet, and extremely effective sentence. It will not only intrigue your prospects, but also push them to ask that next all-important question. "What does that mean?"

You will smile and give them your standard but powerful answer. **"Network Marketing is recommending and promoting what you like**."

Everyday we promote and recommend something. We recommend what hotel to stay at, where to eat and what babysitters to use. We recommend and promote restaurants, movies and video games. We recommend and promote pediatricians, sports teams, and cars. That's Network Marketing and everyone of us does it everyday.

So, how would you explain this to your prospect? Using our old friend the strawberry, you might try something like this:

> Ginny, imagine for a moment that you live next door to me. You went to Safeway to purchase some strawberries and you loved them so much that when you got home, you ran over to my house and said, "Lynn, the strawberries that I got at Safeway are so good you need to get some." Well, I run down to Safeway and buy my own strawberries. And sure enough, they are pretty good. So I go to work the next day and tell my co-workers that they need to go to Safeway and buy some of these great tasting strawberries. All month long I keep doing the same thing. I keep recommending and promoting strawberries to everyone I know.

> Finally, on the 30th of the month, the store manager calls me up and says, "Lynn, you've been so instrumental in helping us make lots of money, and because your recommendations and promotions have created more revenue than all the advertising we pay for, I want to pay you a word-of-mouth advertising bonus check for all of your help."

> That, Ginny, in a nutshell, is what Network Marketing is all about.

As I watch the smile flash across the prospect's face, I know his or her objection has disappeared. I know they now realize exactly what it is we do and how easy it is to do it. Getting paid for what we already do. It's as simple as that.

Stage Four
What about your company?

The next thing your prospect will want to know about is the company he or she may become a part of. Essentially, there are five things your prospect wants to know:

1. What's the name of your company?
2. Where is your company located?
3. How long have you been around?
4. Who's on the management team?
5. Is it a fun place to work?

I recommend that you use company-sponsored brochures or marketing materials to cover these five points. It makes it easy and duplicatable. All you have to do is read. Remember, all you're looking to do is give them just enough facts to help them make an intelligent decision to join. Later on they can get all the fun details—who wears the lab coats and how many square feet in the executive washroom. For now, keep it simple. Stick to the basics.

Stage Five
What kind of products do you have?

Eventually, your prospect will want to know about the products. And while I believe in the enormous health benefits of every product we sell, we could cover this effectively in about five minutes. We don't need to pull out the 37 pages of technical references and data on each product. Not only is it not necessary, but it would undoubtedly send your prospect into a narcoleptic coma. Product information should be left for training.

Of course, what do you do if someone insists on more detailed information about the product? What should you say then? Should you talk about all the benefits of the product— its potency, shelf life or cost? While these are important and valid elements, none of them matter to the prospect. At least not at this stage. All they really want to know is one thing: *does the product sell?*

While they will take you at face value that the product is good and competitively priced, what they really want to know is, if they sign up for their own Network Marketing business, will they have a hot product that people want?

Nobody wants to be in business with a high quality product that people don't want. It's like selling limited edition Ferraris for half a million dollars. It's an incredible product, but how many people are in the market for that? Very few. So while quality is nice, your prospect's main concern is whether or not the product is going to move.

So just how do we respond to questions about the product? We answer their questions honestly and directly, of course. We explain all the types of products we have, how they work and how they can get them, but *we do it with a strong slant towards answering the bigger question -- does the product move? Will it sell?*

We give them specifics about the products, but as we do, we will also inject our stories and testimonials. How you were using such and such product at the gym when someone came up to you and said, "Gee that looks cool, what is it?" And before you knew it, you had an appointment to share the product. Or maybe you'll tell how you went over to your sponsor's house, during which he received three phone calls for one of our products. Stories and testimonials not only show how effective the products are in promoting good health, but also show the high demand for them as well.

Stage Six
Can I do this?

Of all the questions your prospect will ask, probably the one that overshadows them all in importance is this one. Can I do this? If you can't answer it, you can be certain your prospect will go no further on this journey with you. Answer it correctly and you will be able to take him or her anywhere.

Have you ever given a presentation or seen a presentation where the prospect seems so excited and enthusiastic about the company, products and marketing plan, only to tell you at the end of your presentation that it's not for him?

The presenter always scratches his head and wonders, "What the heck happened?"
I'll tell you what happened. Your prospect said, "Great idea, but I can't do it."

You see, it doesn't matter if the presentation is great and the money is fantastic, we can all only do what we think we're capable of doing. And the truth is, the only way we are going to get our prospects to believe they can do it, is to offer them the right training.

It is absolutely imperative—right from the beginning—to let our prospects know we are going to hold their hands and train them every step of the way. We need to let them know we will not allow them to fail. The dialogue you use might sound something like this:

> Ginny, if you're looking at this type of program for the very first time, and you don't know anything about this industry or how to run a home based business, don't worry. Everybody started the same way. We have a training program that will teach you exactly what you need to know to feel confidant. We call it our *Leadership Training Program*. It's a two-part program.

> *Part one is our company training*, which consists of classroom training and a combination of home study materials and on-line tutorials, specifically designed so that you can go through them as fast or as slow as you'd like, all from the comfort of your home. We also have one-on-one mentoring and teleconferencing sessions at least 4 days a week. At these sessions, your telephone becomes your classroom as you learn to ask questions that help you attract and keep top leaders. We refer to this training as Going Back To School.

> *Part two is on the job training.* When you first get started, all you will have to do is set a couple of appointments and your upline-sponsoring mentor will do the rest. He or she will go with you or help you over the phone, sharing your opportunity with your prospect, while you just sit back and observe. Once you are successful and, more importantly, confident, only then will you go out and do it yourself.

Now, wasn't that easy? In one simple explanation, you

have taken all the anxiety, stress and doubt out of the equation. Training is the most important part of the presentation there is. In fact, when you finish explaining the training we offer, maybe 50 to 80% of the people you talk to will immediately say, "Hey that's the business for me. That's what I want to do." And you know why they'll say it? Because they now believe they can do it.

Stage Seven
What kind of industry am I in & how does it work?

Sooner or later, your prospect is going to want to know about the money. They already know they'd like to make some extra cash. And they already know they're willing to give five to seven hours a week to make it happen. They're excited about the products, the marketing, the training and, most definitely, the opportunity to change their lives. Now, they want a few details.

- How much does it cost to get started and what are the benefits?
- What do I have to do to earn all this money?
- And, let's be honest, how much money can I really make?

Let me ask a question. In traditional sales, when do you think the salesperson might start talking about money? In the beginning or the end of the presentation? Probably at the end, just as he was thrown out the door. And because he waited to the end…what was the prospect thinking about during the whole presentation? How much is this going to cost me, right? Unfortunately, the prospect was so concerned with the price, he never listened to all the benefits the salesperson had to offer.

We can't allow this to happen. We need to do things differently. When we start talking about the money portion of our presentation, we need to say right up front how much money it's going to cost to join. We need to get that concern off their mind, so they can sit back, relax and enjoy the rest of our presentation. Your dialogue might go something like this:

> Ginny, one thing you need to understand is that nobody can get involved in this without being referred to the company by an existing distributor. We don't have any retail storefronts, so no one is ever going to find your product line in a store. You have to get involved with someone who is already developing a Network Marketing business. That person is usually called your sponsor or the person that referred you to your company.

> Now, when you join, the company sets you up with your own Network Marketing distribution center. You can start with as many or as few products as you want, whatever you're going to personally use or share and recommend to others. Once you've opened your center, you can begin building your home based business immediately, not only earning your company products at no cost, but also joining the many business partners that are currently earning their weekly advertising bonus checks.

> The first thing you need to do is decide how you would like to get started. As I mentioned earlier, we refer to this as going back to school. Just as you would decide how many credit hours are necessary each year to graduate from college in four years, you need to make the equivalent decision regarding your business. Like in college, if you only take 1 credit

hour, it may take you ten years or more to graduate. However, if you take sixteen credit hours, you would graduate in four years or less. So the level of commitment is in direct proportion to what you are looking to receive. It's entirely up to you.

Now what you have done for your prospect is plain, simple and profound. You have clearly explained that their initial investment is entirely up to them. It's not small or large, but exactly the amount they feel comfortable with. You have put the power back where it belongs—in their hands. And once again, you have made the entire process pressure-free and anxiety-free.

There you have it. Seven simple stages. One powerful presentation. The only thing left for you is to do something with it. Find your prospects and begin. And remember, you're not trying to cram the business down anyone's throat; you're simply trying to help others discover what matters most to them, then show them the way to achieve it.

That takes patience, persistence and a dedication to making your presentation as perfect as it can be. And how do you make it perfect? The same way you get to Carnegie Hall—practice, practice, practice.

*Teamwork is the
ability to work
together toward
a common vision.
The ability to
direct individual
accomplishments
toward
organizational
objectives. It is the
fuel that allows
common people to
attain uncommon
results.*

— Andrew
Carnegie

Chapter Eight
Developing Your Leadership Team

The title of a John C. Maxwell book says it all: "Teamwork Makes the Dream Work." Grasp this simple but powerful concept and you're halfway to achieving success.

Up to this point in the book we've been working on you—what you need to grow, how you can improve, what it will take for you to excel. Now we turn our attention to one of the other most critical factors in determining your success…your team. Whether you know it or not, everyone is part of a team. If you're married, you and your spouse are a team. In your place of employment, you and your co-workers are a team. If you do volunteer work, you're part of a team of volunteers. Even driving down the road, you act as a team in concert with other drivers to ensure everyone's safety. Financial success is no different. If you're going to succeed you need a team. The better the team the greater the results.

In fact, if there's one thing I've learned along this journey of building my home based business, it's that you can't do it alone. Period. Yes, there's a lot of work you can accomplish by yourself. You can spend countless hours writing a vision statement and clearly defining where you are going. You can set your completion dates, live your vision and execute many step-by-step fundamentals alone, but you will never get out of the starting box without assembling your dream team. And you certainly won't get to the finish line. **To do that you need to build a team that is equal to the size of your dream.** Once you clearly understand and accept this fundamental principle, your future will unfold before you like a magical movie, only you're the one writing the storyline.

Of course, putting a team together is one thing. Developing a "leadership" team is another. Anyone can string together some warm bodies and call it a team, but if you're going to truly succeed, you need people who are committed to *delivering on their promises, realizing their visions and doing what it takes to succeed.* Those are the core qualities of a leadership team, and accepting anything less will doom you to failure. I should know. I almost failed myself.

Looking back to the beginning of this journey, I can't help but smile at some of the things I have done and some of the people I have sponsored into my business. I hadn't yet realized I could write my own storyline, create my own future, and I certainly hadn't yet learned the value of developing a leadership team. In fact, I faced such overwhelming difficulties and challenges, not to mention shear desperation, while trying to find my team, I came close to sealing my own failure.

I had no focused idea of where I was headed or whom I needed to help get me there, so I just started taking anyone and everyone with a pulse…anyone who sounded remotely interested. I plugged them into a position and thought that would solve all my problems. It obviously didn't work. The question is, why?

As long as I can remember people have followed me. I've often been told I'm a natural born leader. And because of this, I suppose I had a pretty easy time assembling an army of people who were ready to follow me. The problem was I had no idea where I was going. Not a clue. I had no vision or dream. I was operating on sheer energy and excitement which, like a healthy dose of caffeine, will only take you so far. At the same time, I felt a huge responsibility to all of these people who had chosen me as their leader.

A few years into my journey I began to realize what was happening. I needed to change. I needed direction. I began working on myself, taking ownership for my vision. For the first time I believed in the power of dreams. For the first time I began to realize that maybe I could have it all. And once I gave myself permission to dream and accepted my worthiness my world opened up. I began to sense the possibilities that come from knowing where you're heading. I wrote and rewrote my goals and my dreams. I put together a vision statement and lived it in the present tense as if it was already done. Because it was. My dream was big and I quickly realized that if I was going to achieve this big dream, I would have to assemble a big team. And not just a big team, but the right team. A leadership team. The rest is, as they say, history. My hope with this chapter is that I can save you the years of needless stagnation and aimless wandering I endured by teaching you to develop the right team from day one—a leadership team.

Teamwork Starts With You

Delegating work works, provided the one delegating works, too.
— Robert Half

It all starts with you, which after reading this far into the book, shouldn't come as any big surprise. Now, I know I said this chapter would be about developing your team, but the most important part of that team is you. And, while we covered defining your leadership role in chapter four, it's imperative that we take a brief moment here to discuss your role in the team, specifically your willingness to lead. Because, while we can establish all the qualities and characteristics of a great leader, none of it will mean anything if you're unwilling to lead. And, amazingly, lack of ability is rarely the reason people fail in leadership roles. The main reason people fail is because they simply don't want to lead.

Part of the reason is ego. Even though we all know the power and potential of teamwork, some of us still want to do things by ourselves. Some of us will never admit we need anybody for anything. We erroneously believe we have to do everything ourselves. Look at how many of us will waste time driving around totally lost because we won't stop and ask for directions. Why would we do this? Because asking for directions would mean we needed help and couldn't do it alone.

Another reason we sometimes choose to fly solo is because we're used to it. We've spent our entire lives facing challenges alone and, as a result, don't know how to accept help from others. While this may work to a point, it makes it hard for us to grow and evolve. You can't be truly successful on a large and meaningful scale by trying to tackle everything yourself. It's impossible. Eventually, something has to give and, unfortunately, it's usually our likelihood of success.

Insecurity can also block us from our willingness to lead. We may want to lead, but see it as a weakness to look elsewhere for help. And then there are those individuals who, wanting to be in charge, surround themselves with weak people in order to make themselves feel strong. Of course, this isn't leadership, it's ego gratification and while it may allow them to feel important, it does nothing to help accomplish the team's long-term goals and objectives.

If you recognize yourself in any of these scenarios, it's time to "Get Out Of Your Own Way." You must be willing to get past your own doubts and insecurities if you ever plan to lead a team. And, let's face it—if you ever plan to be successful, you're going to have to lead a team sooner or later. You will have to embrace the concept that your dreams are bigger than your individual capabilities, and that you will never truly accomplish your goals until you plug into the power of the team. Not in this business.

By empowering others, you not only achieve your own goals, you help others achieve theirs as well. It's the highest calling of leadership—helping others improve their lives by helping them realize their potential. But, first, you must be willing to realize your own.

Lead, Follow, Or Do Both

Is there anyone so wise as to learn by the experience of others?
— Voltaire

Okay, so you're willing to lead. That was easy. But, we have to take care of one more piece of personal business before we start putting together our team.

We've all heard Ted Turner's famous line, "Lead, follow or get out of the way." The heading of this section isn't just a kinder, gentler version of Mr. Turner's philosophy, it's a more practical one. To be an effective leader, you must realize you can't do it alone. If you want to become a leader for your team, you must first become a follower. You must find a mentor or a coach who has what you want and is doing what you want to do.

This is a critical step in the team building process and it shouldn't be overlooked. You don't have to reinvent the wheel in creating your own success. You just have to learn to do what you want to do by following the lead of someone who's already done it. Simply find that individual, then follow them around and do what they do, learn from them. The path has already been laid—now all you have to do is follow it. When I clearly decided what I wanted from my USANA business, I immediately went to someone who was already successful in the exact way I wanted to be successful. I asked that person to be my mentor, to teach me the skills of building a team. That's how I became a leader. It was that simple. I now have the most amazing team of individuals connected to their visions and we're all building our futures together. But, I could never have achieved it without the guidance of a mentor. It's not until you're a follower that you will be able to truly lead your own team. The best leaders were always followers first.

Building Your Team

> *Snowflakes are one of nature's most fragile things, but just look at what they can do when they stick together.*
> — Vesta Kelly

So, where does your team come from? How do you materialize these wonderful people who are going to make such a significant contribution to your future success? Remember, we're not just looking for a team, we're looking for a leadership team. Well, I've always found there's no better place to start than the people who already surround you.

Think about the people you know in your life. Think of those who are like-minded and might share a similar vision. These are the people you want to invite to take this magnificent journey with you. Some will be ready to travel, while others will be content to sit it out, at least for the time being. That's fine. Don't judge these people or beat them over the head. Their choices are probably the right choices for where they are at that moment in life. Your energy is much better spent working with people who are willing, excited and, most importantly, ready to go where you're going. It's critical that you keep your eye on the big picture, and this is much easier to do when you surround yourself with like-minded people who embrace your vision for achieving that picture. This is how powerful teams are created. This is how you form a powerful alliance where everyone wins.

As a leader, it is your role to communicate the vision to your team. You're the one who must paint the big picture for your team. The more effectively you do this, the easier it will be to keep the team moving forward. I have found the most effective time to do this "vision painting" is before they join the team. This allows you the opportunity to weed out people who might slow you down later on, just as it allows you to hand pick the people who will be most effective at realizing your vision.

Of course, building your team isn't something you do once then forget about, while you sit back and ride the fast track to success. Every step of the way you'll be looking for new team players. And just as important, you must continuously strive to bring out the best in each person already on your team, recognizing in them what they may not see in themselves. In this way, you're building your leadership team not just by recruiting new people, but by also creating stronger team members out of the people you already have.

One of the best ways to do this, especially when your team members are new, is to properly invest your time in the team. Get to know each and every team member. Do whatever it takes to clearly understand their vision. What are their dreams? Their fears? Challenges? What are they fighting for? Focus your energies on helping them achieve even the smallest success, especially in the beginning. It's amazing how far a "small win" can lift your team up, helping them persevere to the next step.

We also need to toughen up our team by "bullet proofing" them to the negative responses and rejections they may encounter. Surround your individual people with the positive energies of the whole team. Recognize individual efforts at every opportunity, letting them each know what a valuable asset they are to the team. Look for their individual strengths and continuously encourage your team to challenge themselves, letting them know that you are there holding the safety net.

Determine how many hours per week they have to give to their business and coordinate your schedule so you're available as their support, coach, and mentor. Work with them and be their voice until they have their own voice.

Manage their expectations by letting them know they're in school and will be there for several months. Also, you must let them know that while you are their teacher and they are your student, the beauty of the relationship is in that they will earn while they learn.

Finally, as part of their training, you should plug your team into the very first company- sponsored event available. They must never lose site of the big picture, always realizing the enormity of what they're a part of. Do this and, in no time, they will become the teachers looking for their own students, while you continue to look for more students of your own.

Motivation is another key element in building your team. As Ella Wheeler Wilcox once said, "A pat on the back is only a few vertebrae removed from a kick in the pants, but is miles ahead in results." People long for recognition and, often times, will do more for a team than they will do for themselves. I know this first hand, because many years ago my daughter was a competitive swimmer. She would race week after week and always finish fourth or fifth. I knew she was capable of so much more. Not just because a mother always thinks her children can do better, but because I had actually seen her swim faster. Well, one day she was placed on a relay team. When she swam her leg of the relay she tracked the best split time of her competitive career. When I asked her how she could swim that fast in the relay event, but was unable to come even close to that when she was on her own, she replied that the team was counting on her. "I couldn't let the team down, Mom."

As I look back, I realize what a great lesson that was for me. As a leader, I became determined to use this simple "people will work harder for a team than they will for themselves" philosophy as one of the main cornerstones for my success. It's worked for me and it will work for you too. By inspiring people to do better for the team, by motivating them to perform beyond even their own expectations, you can easily lead your team and yourself to success.

When your business is new the first priority is building your team. You want to be able to identify good people, bring them onto your team and create a synergy amongst the team members so they all work well together. But, building the team isn't the only concern. In fact, sometimes I feel it's easier to put the team together than it is to keep it together. To address this reality I'd like to focus on a few key issues that may come up as you're building your team.

Team Troubleshooting

> *If you put good people in bad systems you get bad results. You have to water the flowers you want to grow.*
> — Stephen R. Covey

The first thing we should remember is this: *realizing your vision is a marathon, not a sprint.* There is no way around it—challenges, obstacles and roadblocks will always be a part of the process toward manifesting your dreams. There will always be days when you bang your head on the wall and ask yourself why you ever started this business in the first place. And these are the days when you can't lose site of where you're headed. It's the time when you need to bring out your vision statement and remind yourself *exactly why you started this journey*. With this "big picture" focus, you'll be able to easily identify your problems, devise a solution and get you and your team back on track.

Of course, if it's the team that's the problem, you'll have to deal with that as well. Here are a few solutions to some common team problems.

I've Got the Wrong Team

If you aren't getting the results you're looking for and you've done enough "self" work to eliminate yourself as the problem, you may want to take a look at your team. Perhaps, it isn't the right team to get you where you want to go. You have a big dream, right? Well, is your team big enough to get you there? If the answer is no, you have two choices: One, you can give up your dream or, two, you can find a new team.

When you reach this crossroad, first call a meeting of all team members. This is a last ditch opportunity to sit down together and find out where everyone stands before you go out and start looking for a new team. Often times, it's not the whole team, but just one or two individuals that are the problem. During the team meeting, let everyone know you're getting ready to move forward and are trying to identify where to focus your future energy. Ask your team to tell you how they feel about the progress they're making. Ask them to talk about their past and future commitments. In short, ask them for an honest assessment of where they feel they are in their journey. For many, just asking the questions might refocus their attention and sense of purpose. On the other hand, it might not. In fact, if you were feeling a problem in the first place, inevitably there will be someone in the room—at least one person—who says he is ready to leave and move on to something else. That's okay, let that person go. But, rather than throwing the baby out with the bathwater, hold onto the people who are still committed, but need redirection. It's an easy and powerful way to re-build the foundation of your new team.

At this point, your team might not be the size you need to achieve your dream, but that's fine. At least you know the people you have are 100% committed to the vision. Remember what Mark Twain once said, "It's not the size of the dog in the fight, it's the size of the fight in the dog." You have a committed team. That's enough to move forward. Yes, you still want to build your team to a size that will accommodate your vision, but you now have a strong leaping off point.

Too Many Negative Attitudes

There's not much to talk about here. If you have people on your team with poor attitudes or negative energy, they'll sabotage the entire team...and your vision. To be blunt, get rid of them. Do not allow these people to steal your dreams or the focus of the team. As a leader, it is your responsibility to detach these people as quickly as possible. Negativity attracts negativity, and one bad attitude will spread like a cancer throughout your entire team. Remove that bad attitude and your problem is solved.

Unfortunately, not all negative attitudes are easy to identify. Sometimes they'll make themselves painfully obvious, other times they're more subtle. For instance, there may be individuals who join your team and do absolutely nothing; or individuals who wholeheartedly bought into the dream, then crumbled as soon as they faced their first rejection or challenge; or individuals who are simply unwilling to grow, change and do what is necessary to get to the next step.

And, of course, there will always be individuals who have only joined your team because they wanted to be a part of something. They're not team players. It's all about them and their personal gain. They have the "what's in it for me?" attitude—and with that attitude, it's impossible to plug into the power of the team, so they find themselves isolated and working alone, which makes them unable to achieve the success they're looking for. They haven't realized that the beauty of this industry is that it's only in the giving that you receive.

While all these people are more difficult to identify, it's critical that you do identify them and then act. If you can turn them around, great. If you can coach them back toward their goals, great. But, if you determine they're un-coachable, you need to remove them from the team. Sadly, they may go back to the place where there are no dreams, forced to live out their lives in mediocrity. It's difficult to watch, but remember, it's their choice, not yours. It's their life, not yours. Once you've done all you can to lead people to their dreams, you have to let them go. If you're going to succeed in your dreams, and if you're going to succeed in leading others to theirs, you need to focus on the people who are willing to put out the right effort, with the right attitude.

People Don't Want Success As Much As I Do

One of the mistakes I made in the beginning of my career was thinking I could make success happen for everyone. What I quickly realized was that in many cases, I wanted it more for them than they wanted it for themselves. I was pushing people towards my dream for them, not realizing it wasn't ever their dream in the first place. In short, I was pushing them in a direction they didn't want to go in. The solution here is to realize that everyone has to have their own dream. And, even if you do share the same dream, the timing has to be right in their life for them to go out and fight for their future.

Leadership, and my life, became much easier when I realized it was their life and their responsibility...not mine. Yes, you must teach, you must lead, you must coach, you must inspire, but ultimately it's up to individuals on the team to claim their own dreams.

So, how do you identify this problem? It's not quite as easy as dealing with a negative attitude. These people are a bit harder to sniff out. After all, they're probably going along with the program to a degree, even if their hearts aren't in it. For me, I began to easily identify these people once I found someone who really wanted to succeed. That helped me identify what a great team member looked like, and gave me a comparison for a mediocre team member. Once I had that comparison, mediocrity was as easy to identify as black on white. I never settled for mediocrity in my team members again, and neither should you.

As an example, imagine you have training on a Saturday morning. One team member shows up thrilled and ready to go, even though they had to wake up at 4 a.m. and drive 5 hours to attend. Another team member lives around the block and complains about a 9 a.m. training on a Saturday morning because it's his or her only day to sleep in. Which one shares your vision? Which one is primed to realize his or her own vision? Which one do you want on your team?

Focus your time and energy on the people who are willing to do what it takes to succeed. Understand their vision, then train and mentor them towards realizing that vision.

Personality Conflicts

As your team begins to grow and develop, there will inevitably be conflicts of personalities, jealousies and hurt feelings. This happens even among great team members. As a leader, you can easily be pulled into other people's issues and dramas, but you must avoid this at all costs. Yes, you have to establish the trust of your team by being a good listener, but you must use that trust to guide them forward and past the negatives. Encourage your team to always communicate with those directly involved and remind them all of the big picture. Help them to refocus back on the mission, because time spent in negativity is time taken away from productivity. Too much of this will take the entire team off course.

They're Willing But Unable

You may have people on your team who truly want to succeed and are great team players. They're always there to lend a hand, always eager to attend your training seminars and events, yet they fail to move forward in the business. While these people may lack the ability to get the job done, if their attitude is in the right place, you and your team would be well served by not giving up on them. Let them know you believe in them. Help them to achieve even the smallest successes, for as they do, they will then begin to believe in themselves. Another action you can take is to connect them with a personal mentor or coach. The individual attention may be just what they need to help them shine.

Also, allow them to play in their area of strength. For example, if they're great at graphics, let them design your signage for events and mailers. If they're great with people, let them greet at events and work the room. By helping them succeed in the small things, they'll gain the confidence and ability they need to succeed in the big things.

Attitude

He who has the confidence in himself will lead the rest.
— Horace

As you embark on your journey to success and begin to develop your leadership team, one character trait will benefit you more than any other. Attitude. The law of the universe is clear: If you have the right attitude, you'll attract others with the right attitudes. I once spoke to a group of leaders about building teams, and during my presentation I asked the question, "When you're out there looking for new team members, are you looking for two more of you?" Everyone burst into laughter as a few people shouted out, "No, we're looking for two more of you!"

Their answer both proved my point and the need for people to embrace my point. We attract like-minded people. If we want to attract eager, successful people we must become eager and successful people. As the group indicated, I had attracted them to me. Now, it was their turn to be the people they wanted to be, so they could attract the people they wanted to attract. We must work on ourselves first. We must work on our attitudes. People will always project on the outside how they feel on the inside. Attitude is about how you feel and this largely determines your actions. If you have a positive attitude, people flock to be around you.

If you have a negative attitude, positive people will run to avoid you. If you want to attract positive, become positive.

I have a sign hanging in my office. For the life of me I don't know where it came from, but I keep it because it taught me and continually reminds me of the importance attitude plays in success. The sign says:

A - 1
T - 20
T - 20
I - 9
T - 20
U - 21
D - 4
E - 5

You can see the word attitude, but what do the numbers stand for? Write down the word attitude just as you see it here. Then using the order of the English alphabet assign a number to each letter. For example, "A" is the first letter, so it gets a number 1. "T" is the twentieth letter and gets a number 20. When you add up all the numbers, it confirms the fact that attitude is 100%.

As your attitude improves you begin to attract more positive people into your life. As you attract more positive people, your business begins to move forward. As your business grows and success begins to appear your posture and demeanor begin to change. As your posture and demeanor begin to change people will begin to follow you because they want what you have. They want what you have because you are beginning to want what you have. Are you starting to get the picture?

It's all about you. The success or failure of your business is all about you and attitude has everything to do with that. If there was a party going on with one hundred people in attendance, one person prospecting for team members could walk into that room and come out with ten interested people, while another person could walk in and not one person would be interested. What's the difference? Attitude. All prospects are neutral. It is you who determines whether they are a good prospect or a bad prospect.

If you're not having the results you are looking for, it's time to do a self-check. Remember that thoughts are things. Negative attracts negative. If you feel like your products are too expensive, you will attract people who can't afford them. If you honestly believe success will never happen for you, guess what? It won't. I can't emphasize it enough—the key to developing your team is to become who you're looking for. The person I've become as a result of building this business is worth ten times as much as the money I've made. The people I now bring into my business are in no way similar to the ones I brought in at the beginning. As my business has grown, I've grown as well. It's a wondrous experience and a grand opportunity, and I urge you to embark on it now, starting with developing your leadership team.

Give it everything you can. Your team is already looking to you. They are already investing in you. Find them and give them a good return on their investment. We all have the power to impact our teams in an amazing way, as long as we take the focus off ourselves. As Bill McCartney said, "We have not come to compete with one another. We have come to complete one another."

I'll finish this chapter with two last pieces of advice. The first is to have fun. The second is to catch and embrace the concept that you are only one or two people away from securing your financial future and living the life you deserve. GO OUT AND FIND THEM NOW!

Success is a
journey, not a
destination

— *Ben Sweetland*

Chapter Nine
Driving Across the Finish Line

If Mr. Sweetland is correct, then why are we talking about crossing the finish line? It's a good question. Truth is, success is both a journey and a destination. We planted our dreams and visions firmly in our head with one purpose—we wanted to see them come to fruition, we wanted to see them grow from a tiny wish in our hearts into a concrete, touch-and-feel-it reality. This book isn't about dreams. It's about the realization of our dreams; the slow purposeful fulfillment of the life we had always imagined for ourselves.

Our journey—all the hard work, sacrifice, commitment and risks we take—means nothing if we don't have something to show for it at the end of the day. If we don't have what we set out to achieve. That's the finish line I'm talking about.

Of course, that said, all the triumphs and financial success we achieve as we cross that finish line would also mean nothing if we didn't find purpose, joy, and meaning in the day-to-day journey that brought us to this moment. As I sit in my study today, I can't help but look back on my life so far. I can't help but remember the poverty and loneliness I endured, the emptiness I had once felt so deeply, the longing for something more. And with all the gratefulness in my heart, I also can't help but remember the moment I realized

I could have more…infinitely more. And from that moment to this day, it has been the ride of my life.

Has my liberation been easy? Certainly not. Like any meaningful transformation, it has not been without struggle or effort and even setbacks, but it has been the most fulfilling and rewarding experience in my life. And I'm not talking about the house by the beach, the fancy car or even the cabernet on the balcony. I'm talking about the feeling I get when I wake up each day with the realization that I am living the life I want to live…and that if I made this possible, I can make anything possible. I'm talking about the profound satisfaction I have in helping others find their own peace and freedom. I'm talking about the joy I receive each time I am able to share my life, not with a desk, a boss and a schedule, but with my family and friends. I'm talking about the immeasurable reward that comes into your life when you achieve something with hard work, courage, perseverance and trust.

In short, it is who I have become while I set out to accomplish my dreams that I am most proud of. I can think of no greater joy or accomplishment than knowing you have become the person you always knew you could be. That you reached for the stars and touched them. That is the journey I am talking about. And it has been amazing!

So, yes, success is a journey *and* a destination. We must work toward our goals, visions, and dreams but, in doing so we can never lose sight of the fact that our finish line must not be crossed at the sacrifice of who we are as human beings. We must do better. Try harder. Reach out. Uplift. Inspire. We must do what we can to make a difference in the world we're a part of. It is this *journey of the self* that will give your *sprint to the finish line* it's meaning and purpose.

And to think there was a time I didn't even want to be in Network Marketing. In fact, when I first heard the words, I ran. Actually, I laughed, then I ran. Without knowing it, I had bought into other people's misconceptions regarding Network Marketing. I swallowed their opinions and made them my own: "Network Marketing is for suckers." "You can't make money doing that!" "It's a pyramid scheme." I believed it without knowing why. Truth was, I didn't even know what Network Marketing was. In addition to misjudging Network Marketing, I made a much more critical error. I allowed other people's fears to not only become my own, but to affect my choices. I allowed other people's aversion to change and growth prevent me from being bold...from treading into the uncharted waters that would lead me to new opportunities. Of all the mistakes I have made in my life, that was one of the biggest.

And in doing so, I had unwittingly handcuffed myself to the self-limiting beliefs of others. I had imprisoned myself in a finite world, locked behind four dark walls, with only the promise of a meager, month-to-month paycheck to look forward to. The worst part of it was—like 99% of the world—I had no idea I was trapped inside a prison. Like everyone else around me, this was all I knew. In fact, my circumstances were perfectly matched to my expectations— which were about as low as you could get. I didn't know there could be anything different from the life I was leading, let alone better. And, so I accepted it and came to believe that life was all there would ever be.

Of course, as I've mentioned before, all this changed the day that tiny speck of light came shining through my dark pathetic walls. The day I woke up. You know, of everything we are given in this universe, I believe it is "light" that is our greatest gift. Yes, light. Light is more than the sun or the moon or a lamp that lights up the page we are reading. It is the illumination which guides us to truth. It's a conversation, a book, a song or a word whispered by a stranger. It is a tug in your heart that says, "go this way" or "turn that way." Light can be bold and radiant, a flash of brilliance that knocks us to our knees; or it can be soft and subtle, a glimmer that quietly inspires us. It doesn't matter. Only that it appears and, more importantly, that we pay attention to what it would like to show us. Yes, I will say it again. Light is the greatest gift we have. Without light, we wouldn't be able to see our spouses, our children, families and friends. Not their faces, but what they represent in our lives. You see, light shows us what matters. What we should pay attention to. Light guides us, giving us directions towards freedom and purpose. Light inspires us, making us want to be more than we thought we could be. Most of all, light shows us all the possibilities and potential we have before us.

At least that's what it did for me. When that tiny speck of light came shining through my door years ago, little did I know how it would spread and swell, then multiply, until I could see a whole new world in front of me.

My gratitude for that light has left me forever indebted. It has also left me empowered with the wisdom to know that, like all great gifts, the light grows the more we give it away. In other words, the light we receive in our lives must not stay with us. It must be passed on, so that it can grow and serve others. And, yes, it is prophetic that Network Marketing operates under the same principles of light—take what you know and then pass it along so that others may benefit as well.

That's what I have aimed to do in this book—take what I know and pass it along to those of you who are ready to listen.

And I'll be honest, there is nothing new and earth shattering here, which I firmly believe is the beauty and simplicity of what we're doing in Network Marketing. *We don't need to re-invent the wheel; we only need to use it.* As you embark on your journey, you will be given many suggestions on how to succeed. You will hear talks, listen to tapes, read books. It doesn't matter how it is said or who is saying it, only that you use what you learn to realize your dreams. While I have shared many thoughts on what it takes to succeed in this business—all of them important—I especially hope you will never forget these five power statements of success.

Power Statement #1
Become What You Are Capable Of Becoming

All the wonders you seek are within yourself.
— Sir Thomas Brown

My life has been transformed with this statement, along with the simple idea that the journey to our future begins with the work we do on ourselves. While this is the hardest work of all, it is essential for our success. Truth is, the only thing that stands between you and what you want from life is *you*. It's *your* ability to "make it happen," *your* belief in yourself, *your* patience, *your* hard work and *your* unwavering faith that everything you desire is within reach. And what does that take? It takes you realizing your potential and living up to your capabilities. It takes you being who you were meant to be—your best self. Do that and you will empower yourself to achieve anything you desire. Do that and you will attract the people you need to help make you successful. And, as I've said many times before, this is a business that absolutely requires we attract the right people.

Remember how I said I used to attract all the wrong people? Being a caretaker by nature, I started my career wanting to save the world and USANA was my vehicle. I wanted everybody to join. It wasn't until I spent some really frustrating months trying to push my team up a rope that I figured it out. It was *my* dream for them and not theirs. I wanted this, they didn't. My intentions were out of balance and misguided and, because of this, the commitment was one-sided. Of course, as soon as I started to work on myself, all this changed. As soon as I realized I needed to work on me, to take care of my baggage, my weaknesses and my leadership skills...guess what happened? I became a leader—the leader I knew I was capable of becoming—and, in the process, I started to attract people who were of like mind and values. Now, I no longer look for people who *need* the experience of USANA and Network Marketing, I look for those who *want* it. And what a difference that has made.

While we certainly don't need to recap all the areas where you can improve your life and business, suffice it to say all genuine growth begins with an honest self-evaluation. You need to look deep in your heart and ask yourself one question: what is it that's keeping me from taking the next step? Whatever you lack in your life, find it. Whatever it is that prevents you from moving forward, remove it. In the words of Ralph Waldo Emerson, "Make the most of yourself, for that is all there is of you."

Power Statement #2
Take Action Quickly and Convincingly

The wise man does at once what the fool does finally.
— Baltasar Gracian

When you set out to actually build your dream and create your vision, don't hesitate. Believe me, it's too painful to do it slowly. Decisive and concrete action works miracles. It also prevents procrastination from rearing its ugly head.

Personally, once I had done the work on myself, once my vision was in place and I was fully committed to the journey, I charged out of the starting block and never looked back. I wanted to get done as fast possible in order to enjoy the benefits as soon as possible. I created massive momentum by sponsoring, training and duplicating my efforts. Of course, I knew in my heart that this was more than just a fast track to success, this was my fight for freedom and I was no longer willing to wait for what I knew I deserved.

I took a lot of criticism for the amount of time and energy I put into building my business. I have to admit that it became a huge priority in my life. I didn't have the balance that everyone kept telling me I needed, rationalizing that all the work I was doing was only so that I would have the balance later. Truth is, I came to realize that balance and momentum don't always go together and while the momentum took on a life of its own, the balance seemed to slip further and further away. In the early days, I had to constantly evaluate what the goal was and the price I was willing to pay for it. I think that is the key for each of us. While I may say to you "jump out of the gate and do it fast," you will have to decide for yourself what price you're willing to pay for your success. It takes time to build your business and time is finite. It must come from somewhere else…and that something or someone always pays the price for it.

There were so many nights I couldn't spend with my husband because they were spent at meetings in other people's houses, and so many weekends I couldn't spend walking the beach because they were spent doing trainings.

They were tough times for us, but we never lost sight of the vision, which is the lifestyle we now enjoy. This business is all about choices, priorities, communication, and commitment. Make sure you and the individuals in your life are on the same page and that you all fully realize the sacrifices your journey will require.

From the very beginning, I made a conscious decision to devote **ninety seriously committed days** to getting my business jump-started and off the ground. I was working a full time job and after my workday finished at 5 p.m., I had one hour to get home, get a bite to eat and be ready for a 7 p.m. meeting that I had set up. I decided that for those ninety days I was going to have an appointment every evening Monday through Friday, and that I would train every Saturday. The pace was exhausting but I kept focused on the vision statement hanging in my office and I knew I could do it. Fact is, I believe you can do anything for ninety days if you set your mind to it.

And, like I said, I wanted to build my business quickly and get the momentum started, which is always the hardest part. Gathering your momentum is like being strapped into a roller coaster seat. You creep slowly upward and upward, until finally you peak at the top, then the speed picks up and, well…everything else just takes care of itself. All you have to do is hang on.

I won't lie to you. Those first ninety days were the toughest of my USANA journey, but they are the days that have given me my biggest payoff. They set me up for where I am today.

Once again, I have to ask you, how badly do you want this? Are you ready to draw your line in the sand? Are you ready to strap yourself into that roller coaster and hang on for the ride of your life? Do it fast and I guarantee you'll never regret it.

Power Statement #3
Share the Ride. Share the Wealth.

If you would lift me up you must be on higher ground.
— Ralph Waldo Emerson

There is an old Buddhist saying that goes, "if you light a lamp for someone, it will also brighten your path." In Network Marketing and especially with USANA, we are here to help others succeed, which in turn helps us succeed. It's not a matter of using people or expecting others to do our job, it's a mutually beneficial relationship of like-minded individuals helping each other get where they all want to go.

I am always amazed at how much secrecy and silence there is in other businesses. It's as if people don't want to share their ideas, strategies and resources to get ahead. It borders on hoarding and it's completely counterproductive. Unfortunately, it's a product of that same finite, "not enough to go around" mentality we talked about in earlier chapters— "I can't help you succeed, because there'll be less success for me." Nothing could be further from the truth. There is no poverty consciousness in Network Marketing (and life for that matter). There is enough for all of us. Believe me, *each and every one of us can have it all.* And the faster we realize this, the faster it will materialize in our lives. What's more, sharing our journey, success and wisdom with others is not only good business—it's good living. Truth is, one of the biggest blessings of this journey has been that each member of my family has joined me on this USANA path to freedom. After many years of disconnected lives, we are now joined by a common vision of health and financial freedom. And considering how far apart we once were, it is amazing.

When I was just 16 years old my father died of cancer. For two years, I had watched him suffer, struggle and lose to the disease that would leave my mother a widow, alone to raise six children. My mom had lost the person she loved most in the world, while my brothers, sister and I had lost our hero. It not only devastated our family, it tore us apart. We were all so lost in our own grief and pain that we somehow allowed the family to drift. Slowly, we all began to go our separate ways, each of us living in isolation from the other. In fact, when I left home my youngest brother was only 4 years old. I didn't even know him. My sister was 9 and I had three other brothers as well. Eventually, one by one, we all found a way to escape the pain. We all ran for our lives.

It was a tragic time for us all. The separation we felt from one another was enormous and, who knows, it might have lasted forever, if weren't for the gift of USANA. I'll spare you the details of the sappy reuniting, but let me tell you this…we are all together today. We are all involved and connected again as business partners, siblings, and friends. What's more, we have each made a pact that not one, but all of us will know what it feels like to cross the finish line. I now talk to my siblings every day. We are here to support and encourage each other until we are all achieving the goals we set out to achieve. We share our hard times and we share our successes. But mostly, we just laugh and cry over the amazing growth we have experienced, each of us grateful for the personal development we have had to go through to bring our businesses and lives to where they are today.

As I am writing the last few pages of this book, I am looking up at a photograph of my Dad smiling down on me. It is the last picture ever taken of him and I am feeling his love, encouragement, support and pride for who I have become. I know if he were here today, he'd be overjoyed to see his family back together again, sharing their journey toward the life he would have wanted us to live.

We should never forget that business, like life, is something you share.

Power Statement #4
Quitting is Not an Option

> *Our greatest glory is not in never falling, but in rising every time we fall.*
> — Confucius

The journey across the finish line will never be one without scrapes, bumps and, worse, temptations to quit. In fact, I don't care how wonderful and lucrative the opportunities you're involved with are, there will always be that urge to pack it in and walk away. The greatest entrepreneurs in the world have all wanted to quit at one time or another. In fact, the desire to quit comes with our desire for growth. Changing the status quo is never easy. It takes stamina and persistence. And to be perfectly honest, there are some pretty good reasons why we would want to quit in the first place.

You may find yourself with a spouse that doesn't support you or family members that do all they can to sabotage you. Even your friends will sometimes try to steal your dreams. They will question your choices, dump cold water on your successes and highlight your failures.

And, of course, you may also want to quit because it's just plain hard. Maybe you're working full time, two jobs, with a family, kids and a social life. There's just not enough time in the day to pull it off and you're stressed, wondering if it's all worth it. Well, I can't make it easier for you, but I can absolutely promise you that when you cross that finish line you will look back and know that the journey was worth the price you paid.

Of course, probably the biggest reason we quit is because we don't get immediate results. We come in all excited and gung-ho at the prospect of starting our own Network Marketing business. We are energized with daydreams of fancy cars and mansions on the beach. But, as soon as someone doesn't respond in a positive manner, we are cut off at the knees. We take it personally and make it all about us. We end up feeling rejected, which brings up old, childhood "you'll never amount to anything" insecurities or it launches us into a self-fulfilling spiral of doubt. We tell ourselves we can't do it.

Well, guess what? You *can* do it! You just need to get tougher. And you can start by going back and working on yourself. Get rid of the mental baggage that keeps you stalled in your tracks; get rid of those old beliefs that someone else put you in your head, then get back in the game. And when you get back in the game, take your vision statement with you.

And, remember, your journey is a marathon, not a sprint. It takes time. While you may not be where you want to be now, you can be sure of one thing—the vehicle you have chosen is your path to freedom. If you give it time and allow it to work its magic, you'll get where you want to go. The vehicle works. USANA works. You just have to be willing to hang in there for as long as it takes.

I believe that so many people fail in this industry because they stop just a bit short of the finish line. They get so close, then allow themselves to run out of gas just as the finish line is in sight. It's like drilling for oil. You drill and you drill and find nothing. What do you do? Do you quit? Maybe, if you're speculating. But, what if you know there is oil down there. You've seen the oil (or in the case of USANA, the success stories.) You keep drilling, that's what you do. You drill and then drill some more. And if you still hit nothing, you take another look at your vision statement, then remind yourself that there is something down there…something that can change your life forever, then you go back and drill some more.

Does it matter that it might take 6 months, a year or two years to find it? It shouldn't. In fact, you should be able to drill for 10 years to reach it, especially if you know that it will free you up for the rest of your life.

I understand there will be days when you'll question everything there is about this business. It's only natural. On those days, I would urge you to answer these questions as well: *Are you happy with the life you are now living? Do you have the financial security you want? Do you have enough time to spend with your family, friends, or even yourself? Are you settling for a job that you don't really love?* If your answer was *no* to any of these questions, then keep drilling.

Power Statement #5
Always Remember the Vision

If you can dream it, you can do it.
— Walt Disney

A couple of years ago, a group of us were having dinner and I asked each person to stand and share with the room what their goals for the future were. My brother David stood up, said that he would like to retire and then quickly sat down. Someone in the room called him back up and asked him to put a date to it. They said unless you have a date, it's just a dream.

David thought about it for a moment, then stood up and softly announced, "January, 2005 will be my retirement."

Well, the look on my sister-in-law's face was priceless. She almost fell off her chair. She had no idea what he was going to say. David's date had been set and his vision was intact. You could see it in his eyes. He knew without a shadow of a doubt that he would be retiring in January of 2005.

After that, incredible things began to happen. As usual, David continued to work on building his business, but this time it was different. Every time he ran into an old friend or acquaintance and they would ask him how his USANA business was doing, he would say the same thing. "Well, I'm going to be retiring in January of 2005."

To say he got a few looks would be an understatement. He was 44 years old and here he was telling folks that he would be retiring shortly. He didn't exactly know how he was going to do it and they didn't ask, but they immediately wanted to see what he had to offer. They wanted to hear his story. See his plan. They wanted to be a part of it. They weren't just following David, they were following his vision as he saw it. He began to attract the most gifted and talented people to his team—creative, bold and inspiring individuals. David took them under his wing and began to help them establish a vision of their own.

At the same time, his current associates were so excited about what he was accomplishing that it renewed their faith in themselves and their own dreams. Soon, they began to flourish in their own businesses. It wasn't long before David's business took on a life of it's own. Momentum took over, until he was soon creating the vision he had set up. And, well, you can imagine the rest.

David has since fired his boss and he now has a hugely successful business that allows him to stay home with his wife and four beautiful children. He is living his dream and he is doing because he had the vision to see it long before it happened.

That is the power of vision I have come back to again and again. By now, you all hopefully know what to do. You know where you want to go with your business. You know what you want to achieve, when you want to achieve it and the price you're willing to pay for it. You can feel it, touch it and believe it with every fiber of your being. Most importantly, you feel worthy to bring it into your life. Now, it's time to take that vision statement and start living it.

The gap between your vision statement and reality is closer than you think.

Your Best Life

> *Write on your heart that every day is the best day of the year.*
> — Ralph Waldo Emerson

As we come to the end of this journey together, my desire for each and every one of you is simple: I wish that you find and live your best life. The life you were born to live.

We are put on earth to make a difference. We don't do this by accident, but by choice. We make a difference because we decide to make a difference. It begins in our hearts, with a conscious choice to create lives we can be proud of—lives of purpose, joy, and fulfillment. We don't have to take life the way it comes to us. We can design life to come to us the way we want it…on our terms.

My life has been so dramatically changed as a result of this journey that I find it impossible to keep going without giving back, without passing on the light I was given so many years ago.

My thoughts are with of all of you who are out there struggling, trying to find your way to a better life. I hope you will take my next, carefully chosen words to heart:
YOU DESERVE THIS AND YOU CAN DO IT!
Together we can do it.

We're not here merely to make a living. We are here to enrich the world with a finer spirit of hope and achievement. We are here to dream and we must never doubt that a small group of thoughtful, committed, and focused people can change the world. In fact, it is the only thing that ever has.

I want to share a poem with you that has been hanging in my office since the day my USANA journey began. These words guide my journey and offer me hope and encouragement in the darkest days. I hope it offers you the same.

The Comfort Zone

Author Unknown

I used to have a comfort zone
Where I knew I couldn't fail
The same four walls of busy work
Were really more like jail.

I longed so much to do the things,
I'd never done before.
But stayed inside my Comfort Zone
And paced the same old floor.

I said it didn't matter
That I wasn't doing much
I said I didn't care for things
Like diamonds, furs and such.

I claimed to be so busy
With the things inside my zone
but deep inside I longed for
Something special of my own

I couldn't let my life go by
Just watching others win
I held my breath and stepped outside
To let the change begin

I took a step and with new strength
I'd never felt before
I kissed my Comfort Zone "good-bye"
And closed and locked the door

If you are in a Comfort Zone
Afraid to venture out
Remember that all winners were
At one time filled with doubt

A step or two and words of praise
Can make your dreams come true
Greet your future with a smile
Success is there for you!!!

Even in my darkest moments, I knew I wasn't put on earth
to play it small. I knew I had my own destiny to reach and
many roles to play—daughter, wife, mother, grandmother,
sister, friend, entrepreneur, speaker, writer and, of course,
teacher. I am blessed for each and every experience, for they
have all helped me become what I am today.

I want you to know I have never been more proud to be
a part of an industry or a company than I am with Network
Marketing and USANA. I am privileged to share what I have
learned; to pass on the light I was blessed to have been given.
I am honored in knowing that I have played even a small part
in helping you build your futures.

I wish you all the love, joy and prosperity that I know
you will create.